DON'T ASK ME, ASK

THE AUTOBIOGR/
MIKE BRACE CBE I

CW00872106

Disability is a state of mind, my state, and your minds!

You can't change my state, but hopefully, I've said something that has changed your mind?

To my wife Mo:

"Anyone who can put up with me for over 40 years
deserves a medal"!

The second part of Mike Brace's autobiography, following his life since the first book, "Where There's A Will" was published by Souvenir Press, in 1980.

For further information visit www.mikebrace.co.uk

ISBN-13: 978-1540352439
ISBN-10: 1540352439

Edited by John Duffy
Images and cover design by Bill Craddock

Printed by CreateSpace

Contents

Chapter 1

This Is Your Life

1976-81

When Eamonn Andrews greeted me outside Bush House, the home of the BBC's World Service, and said those immortal words:

"Mike Brace, sportsman and social worker, "this is your life", I was filled with a mix of emotions. My first reaction was one of surprise and disbelief, and even suspicion, i.e. was it really Eamonn or a friend trying to be funny and putting on an Irish accent? Then, confirmation came from Brian Johnston whom I was there to meet, so it must be true!

After the shock wore off and we were on our way to the studio to record the programme, I also had another thought, I was only 31 and appearing on "this is Your Life", was that it then? Had I done everything that I was going to do with my life?

I thought back on the day I had just had prior to being grabbed for "This is Your Life". The day had been a bit hectic and of course I did not have any inkling of what was to come later. When you are an ordinary individual you never expect or dream that something like "This is Your Life" will ever involve you! Looking back after the event I should have smelt a rat.

On the previous Monday I received a phone call from my friend Robbie, who was the Metro blind cricket team's Captain, to say that he now had to work on the following Wednesday when Metro were due to have their

Cricket AGM. I offered to Chair the meeting but he was very insistent that he wanted to be there and that the meeting was cancelled. I remember putting the phone down and thinking, the guys are going to be really hacked off with the meeting being cancelled, just because Robbie couldn't make it. A few minutes later the phone rang again, and on answering it, I found that it was Brian Johnston, the broadcaster, cricket commentator and Metro's President. He was asking if I could by any chance help him out by doing an interview about blind cricket for the World Service of the BBC? He said that he knew it was short notice but was I free on this coming Wednesday evening? I, like the idiot I am, said, "that's really spooky, until about 3 minutes ago I would have had to say no, but my Club's cricket meeting has just been cancelled so I am now free".

Brian went on to say that we might have a bite to eat afterwards and tactfully suggested that perhaps I should wear something a bit smarter than my usual social worker's uniform of jeans and jumper! He then astounded me by saying he would send a car for me. I say I was astounded, as anyone who worked with the World Service in those days, knew that they had no budget for things like cars, and barely had enough money to make the programmes!

I still didn't suspect anything; well you wouldn't, would you?

At work the day after the phone call from Brian, my Team Clerk at the social work office said, "it will be great to see your guide Rolf again won't it?" I thought, what an odd thing to say, as I wasn't due to see Rolf, my skiing guide until I went training in Norway the following March! Lesley recovered well and said "... Oh, in March when you go skiing".

I again thought it was a bit odd, but again did not suspect anything. On the morning of my supposed meeting with Brian Johnston I took Mo a cup of tea in bed (more about her role in the subterfuge later), kissed her and set off to visit a large children's home in Hornchurch. I had qualified as a social worker in 1976, worked for Tower Hamlets Local Authority and had 12 children and young people in care on my caseload placed there. I thought, as it was near to my home, that I would stand a fighting chance of being on time for my driver at 5.30 that evening.

As I left Mo I asked her what she had planned for the day, and she had replied nothing special, and said she planned to laze around and relax. Imagine my surprise therefore when I popped back home within 3 minutes of leaving, having forgotten something, to find Mo up and downstairs rushing around like a maniac! I had always prided myself on being able to tell when Mo was hiding something or telling porkies, but not on that occasion. She had apparently known for over a year that "This is Your Life" was considering featuring me as a subject but thought they had gone off the idea. Then six weeks earlier from the day in question, (the maximum time they thought anyone could keep such a secret), they had phoned her and said that it was all systems go for the 4th of November. A researcher had visited and gone through my address book and asked Mo who she thought I would like to be on the programme. A number of guests had then been contacted and had agreed to appear.

So off I trotted to work, still none the wiser, and met with the kids, the bit of my job I really enjoyed. I was compassionate to the plight the kids found themselves in and passionate that someone, me in this case, should try and make a difference in their lives. I had no idea then if the kids knew how I felt and it has been both humbling and highly emotional to have been contacted recently, over thirty years later, by a number of the kids, now in their forties, to say how much I meant to them and why, having gained access to their records, they felt the need to contact me.

I remember rushing home, after my visit, late as usual, (I think social workers have almost a pathological inability to be on time for anything) to find the driver Jim, waiting for me. I think I was about 15 minutes late, and thought that it was no big deal as all the programmes at the World Service were recorded, so it wouldn't matter if we were a few minutes late. I was due there for 6.30 and as the time was then 5.45, and I still had to change, there was no way we would do the 15 mile journey in the rush hour in 30 minutes!

I put on my best trousers and a shirt which Mo had left out for me (she was not in, funny that!), I strolled out to Jim the driver, and was put in the back of quite a posh car for a cab! We then set off at a hundred miles an hour, I kid you not. Talk about thinking of everything, Jim kept giving updates over the car radio to the programme organisers. As the World Service was run by the BBC and "This is Your Life" was an ITV programme, they had even changed the car's call sign to BBC 1! I still didn't tumble and just felt overwhelmed and honoured that my progress to the World Service was thought to be of such importance to warrant five minute updates via the car radio! We made it in 30 minutes from Hornchurch to the Strand and I rushed to get out of the car on arrival, with relief, only to find that I was child locked in! Brian was there to meet me and as I eventually struggled out of the car, I was aware of him saying something about wanting to introduce me to a very old friend of his, Eamonn Andrews. As I was thanking the driver, I then heard Eamonn saying, that he wanted to meet me "for a very special reason, because, "Mike Brace, social worker and sportsman, this Is Your Life".

My honest first thoughts were that someone was taking the p...s and was putting on a phoney Irish accent. My second reaction was one of complete shock and after uttering "you're joking, you're joking", I was completely lost for words (which for anyone that knows me is almost unheard of!). I was then put back in the car I had just climbed out of, with Brian Johnston in the front passenger seat and Eamonn next to me in the back. I was aware of Brian saying something like, "I'll tell you more about what's going to happen when we get to the theatre around the corner in the Aldwych."

Eamonn was saying something like,

"You're surprised then?"

I just sat there in a state of complete shock and then, I am ashamed to say, did the smelliest fart I have ever experienced! One of the biggest moments in my life and my lasting memory was the obnoxious smell wafting out of my trousers! It was so bad that Brian and Eamonn both hurriedly wound down their windows, and stuck their heads out!

Another lasting memory is us driving down the strand with Brian and Eamonn's heads out of the window and Eamonn saying whilst coughing his lungs up, "I can see (cough, cough,) you were (cough cough) surprised"!

Poor Jim, the driver just had to choke! I just sat there apologising and thanking my lucky stars that it was only a fart!

We arrived at the theatre and I was ushered into a dressing room. I was told that the recording would start at exactly the time the programme would be broadcast which left about 40 minutes to relax and get changed into a suit. I said that I didn't have a suit (still in shock of course) and Brian said that they had a smart brown suit there, with a Round Table badge on it. They must have got a bit worried that I would not cope with the actual programme when I responded, "Oh, I've got one like that at home"!

Of course it was my own suit that Mo had brought up to the theatre that afternoon. Suitably attired I sat there and was introduced to the sound engineer who wanted to put a small radio mike down the front of my trousers. I then had a moment of panic. Suppose my outbreak of flatulence reared its ugly head, just as they were doing a sound check?!

I then found myself having a few minutes on my own to reflect on what had, and was going to, happen.

Who would they bring on as my guests were my initial thoughts? Would I remember them if they were from my distant past? Could I keep my emotions in check or would I cry like a baby?

I had gone blind aged 10 following a firework accident when someone had concealed a banger in a black medicine bottle which I had picked up and which exploded in my face. Would it be the kids with me when I had the accident? Would it be the boys that had concealed the firework in the bottle? Surely not!

I then went to a special school for the blind in Wandsworth. Would some of the guests be my teachers from school?

I had continued my love of sport at the school and developed an interest in folk music. Would someone from my school sports teams be on the programme, or members of my school and later folk groups be there?

I then studied as a shorthand typist and worked in the Civil Service. I realised after 2 weeks in the job that I wasn't very civil or anyone's servant, and studied hard to move on. Surely nobody from the typing pool would be trotted out!

Having got my 2 "A" levels whilst working in the Civil Service, I trained as a social worker at the North London Polytechnic. After a shaky start there, (with me thinking that somewhat uncharitably my fellow students were a bunch of sad weirdoes), I had a great time. Would fellow students be marched on? Oh God, I hoped not, as they might have a tale or two to tell!

I then started work as a social worker in Tower Hamlets. Whilst I worked as a generic social worker i.e. with adults as well as children, I found that my empathy and skill, to some extent, was relating to, and engaging with, young people. I remembered some of the funny situations I had been in, and the amusing comments from the parents and children I had worked with. Presumably it wouldn't be any of them as that would be too sensitive?

As well as embarking on a social work career, I had also discovered skiing in the early 1970's, and had represented Great Britain at the first Paralympic Winter Games in Sweden in 1976, and the second Winter Paralympics in Norway in 1980. Would someone from my competitive sporting activities be brought on, and if so, who?

I then thought about my family. Wait until I saw Mo! My mum and her sister had had a colourful past with 9 husbands between them! They deserved to be on the programme as subjects, but perhaps they had too many skeletons in the cupboard! What would they say?

My brother John had taken a bit of a backseat in the family when I had my accident, with our mum focussing a lot of her attention on me during the weekends when I was home from boarding school. Would he take this moment to mention how he felt?

I had some great friends, who would they select to come on and recount those embarrassing moments that I had seen revealed on other "This Is Your Life" programmes?

They always had a final guest that you hadn't seen for years, would they bother to go to that much effort for me and if so, who could it be?

I had begun after dinner speaking some 2 years earlier, would it be someone from the Round Table, where it had all started, I hoped not!

My musings were soon interrupted by a knock on the door and Eamonn Andrews saying the time had come to start the programme. I had been told that we were to walk into the theatre from the front, walk through the auditorium and then go up a few steps onto the stage. I learned later from Mo that the producers had been worried that I would not manage the walk, or to climb the stairs, and they had seriously considered starting the programme with me on the stage with the curtains opening on Eamonn and me! However when she pointed out that I was a Paralympic athlete and was probably more able to manage the stairs than Eamonn was, they relented and agreed for me to enter the auditorium the same as anyone else. I had given Eamonn a quick lesson in sighted guiding i.e. letting me hold his arm rather than him grabbing me in a vicelike ex boxers grip and carrying me up the stairs!

We set off and I was hit immediately by the noise of 500 people clapping. I hadn't even considered the fact that there would be a live audience. When I did, I thought as we walked through, how disappointed they would be when they realised that I was not anyone famous.

I then sat, for the next 30 minutes, in a dream, as one after the other special and important people from my past and present were brought on to say funny or flattering things about me.

Brian Johnston was on the stage to start with and then they brought Mo on. Mo is one of the shyest people I have met and I was totally amazed that:

a. she had kept this immense secret for weeks and

b. she was standing on stage with me in front of 500 people speaking to Eamonn.

I gave her hand a squeeze, called her a cow and said I would have words with her later!

Then came my mum with Ron (husband no. 4), my aunties, brother and his wife plus my step brother and step sister with their partners.

So far, so good I thought.

They then brought on several friends and teachers from school and from my folk group which I sang with, when I left school.

One of the friends recounted an occasion when he and I went to a naturist camp to raise money for our sports club and when, as my friend Allan put it, "reaching out to shake hands took on a whole new meaning"

I then was amazed when they brought on Charlie Magree the boxer, whom I had met when he opened my club Metro's athletics meeting. Having just got over the shock of Charlie, they then mentioned my passionate support for Tottenham Hotspurs and brought on my hero of the day, Ossie Ardiles. When I thought it couldn't get any better, they brought on my childhood Spurs hero, Bobby Smith the England and Spurs centre forward. When I had my accident and was lying in bed in Moorfields Eye Hospital with pads over my eyes, and the doctors were trying to save my sight, Bobby and another legendary Spurs player, Danny Blanchflower, came in to visit me.

The surprises weren't over yet. Next to appear were my two ski guides, Guttorm and Rolf, both from Norway. I couldn't believe that they had flown people over from Norway just for me!

With still a few minutes to go, I thought there can't be anyone else surely?

I had developed an interest in trying somewhat unusual and potentially challenging sports, one of which was Para kiting. This is where you go up on a parachute behind a land rover or boat and fly through the air. They therefore brought on my parakite instructor Brian, who had a bit of a special place in my regard in that he had not been daunted by my request to try something new, and enabled me to have an experience I have never forgotten.

When I was about 14, we used to go to a caravan in Great Yarmouth for our holidays. The highlight of the week was when we went to the show in the theatre, and on one occasion we went back stage to meet the performers. Marty Wilde was a big star then and the Tornadoes were a popular group, and the light relief was supplied by someone named Rolf Harris. He and I got on really well and he drew a picture of his face on the back of an autograph card, which he then proceeded to raise up with his pen to provide me with an image of his face that I could feel. I was immensely impressed by this and we corresponded for several months afterwards from wherever he was around the world. Imagine my surprise then when the next sound I heard was the didgeridoo and the next guest was Rolf Harris. He remembered the drawing he had done all those years ago and gave me another one he had drawn for the occasion. My emotions were in turmoil but there was more to come.

Eamonn then turned in the script to my work as a social worker and started to mention the family of 2 girls and a boy who were the first children

I had taken into care. Their mother was dying of multiple sclerosis and their father had given up trying to cope. He had abandoned them by giving up his flat, and the children's only home, whilst they were on a school journey! I had to meet them from the coach and take them to see their mother in hospital and then to a children's home in Mill Hill. They were aged about 14, 12 and 10 at the time and their plight really got to me. My heart leapt and my stomach went over when onto the stage came Mary, Jackie and Michael now aged 19, 17 and 15. They said some wonderful things about me, and what I meant to them, and, I'm afraid the tears started to flow. Apparently even Eamonn was crying! There was so much waterworks that a viewer wrote to me afterwards to say, "I thought it was disgusting that the programme didn't provide anyone with tissues".

So my emotional roller coaster was over my surprise guests had arrived and I was waiting for Eamonn to give me the red book and say those immortal words - but, he wasn't finished.

Through my tears I heard him then talk about how 2 friends and I had been inseparable as youngsters. Alan had already come on as a guest and Keith, the third of the musketeers had emigrated to New Zealand the day after he got married some 8 years earlier.

The tears started to flow again when I heard a voice with quite a strong New Zealand accent say, "and you don't think a mere 12,000 miles would stop me from being here do you?"

I nearly didn't hear Eamonn say, "Tonight, Mike Brace, This Is Your Life"!

Tears were flowing, the audience were on their feet, and I was hugging everyone, which was a bit difficult because I had a bloody great red book in my hands!

Eamonn then came and relieved me of the book, not because he was aware of my need to hug more easily, but because there is nothing in the Red Book at that stage other than his script, and possibly a cheese sandwich in case he got hungry during the show.

When I had watched the show previously Eamonn had referred to the after show party, and sure enough they had arranged one for me too.

As well as the guests that had appeared on the show, about 60 other guests had been invited. The emotional turmoil started again with yet more people from my past hugging and kissing me. Friends from my club Metro were there; Danny Blanchflower, the football legend was there; my scout master from school greeted me, and I thought I had best take it steady when the drink started to flow, as I wasn't sure I could keep my emotions in check much more.

At about 9 o'clock one of the producers took me aside and said that they had arranged for 2 Daimler Limos to take me and about 16 guests to a restaurant for a meal. I must have looked a bit worried because he then asked me if that was all right? I asked if the restaurant was already booked, as if not, couldn't we stay at the theatre and carry on with the party. I am not sure if this was the first time a subject of the programme had asked this, but he reluctantly agreed.

At midnight, having drunk the bar completely dry about 18 of us packed into the 2 limos that had been waiting all the time, and set off across London to my home in Hornchurch.

I have a slightly fuzzy memory of drunken guests leaning out of the car window and telling the passengers in the cars next to us that we had been on "This is Your Life". Having got home we then started to party in earnest. I remember waking up about 8 a.m. and thinking firstly, "Was it a dream?" and secondly, "Oh God, I'm late for work!"

Chapter 2

Disabled and Working: Should I be Any More Ambitious?

1981/82

As already mentioned, at the time of the recording of This Is Your Life and its eventual screening in January 1982, I was working as a social worker in Tower Hamlets. I was both respected and liked, but I had been a social worker for five years and felt that perhaps it was time for a new challenge i.e. trying to get a job as a Manager.

An opportunity came up to do this, when a colleague managing one of the social work teams went off sick and I was asked to act up in his place. It was not all smooth sailing however. I had the skills needed, but experienced some resentment from a staff member who found it difficult to accept that someone with a disability had been asked to do the job and not her. I think she also doubted my abilities and wouldn't accept that I could perform all the tasks necessary without imposing on the good will of the staff.

Having experienced management for a few weeks it gave me the confidence to, at least try, to get a permanent job in management. Just as I came to this conclusion, I was contacted by a manager from a children's home in which I had 2 difficult young girls placed. He was setting up a new regional assessment unit for adolescent girls in Hackney and asked me if I would consider applying for one of the unit Manager posts? The centre would have a closed prison unit and three open assessment units. The girls placed there would come from all over London and would be at the upper end of the difficult to help and control spectrum. Part of the attraction was the fact that the unit was in Hackney, the London Borough I was born in and lived in until I was 19.

I discussed with Mo whether I should apply. The minuses were: the journey would be a nightmare – 2 tube trains and a mainline train to get there and back; the job would involve shift work, including sleep-overs; and, I wondered whether I would have the same flexibility to pursue my skiing activities?

I had a safe job, where I was liked and I think respected, and had developed a level of professional competency which might be different from that needed in the new job. My disability, in the professional context of my social work job, was largely either accepted or felt to be irrelevant. Possibly the biggest deterrent from changing was that I had become extremely attached, (perhaps too attached), to the youngsters I had been working with, some for many years. I was sure they would cope and not miss me, but I knew I would miss them very much!

Despite this long list of negatives, I decided that I would apply for the Manager's post, and was excited, anxious and flattered that I was shortlisted, and then got through to a final interview. Nothing however prepared me for the interview itself.

The Chair of the Panel was an Assistant Director in Social Services and the other Panel members were the Unit Head and a senior personnel officer. I had prepared myself for the interview in that I had reviewed my experience of working with adolescent girls and had some answers ready regarding the issues and challenges. I had gone over my limited role as a manager and thought I could use my experience of being managed well, and badly, to my advantage, and could bluff my way through the range of managerial tasks I had performed when overseeing the social work team. I felt fairly confident therefore entering the interview room but nothing, in the end, prepared me for the first question. The Chairman of the interview panel, having introduced the other Panel Members opened the questioning with:-

"I was against short listing you, but was persuaded otherwise by my colleagues, can you convince me why they were right and I was wrong"?!

Very "equal opportunities" I am sure!

I sat there for a few seconds, literally speechless, and then launched into a list of my skills and abilities, and after five minutes he said, "Ok, ok, you've convinced me".

As it happens, I had no idea if I could cope with managing in that type of environment, and more importantly, how the girls would see and cope with my disability. I was warned that violence was likely to be a common occurrence, and I had my doubts how I would cope with this aggression. I was sure that some of my potential staff colleagues would have similar doubts.

The opening question was therefore like a red rag to a bull, and I was bloody sure I wasn't going to give in easily to a blatant example of prejudice and narrow mindedness. It might of course, have been the intention that the question was a deliberate ploy to get my temper up. Well if it was, he succeeded!

The rest of the interview went much more traditionally and I left the interview feeling that I had done the best I could in the circumstances.

I must have done ok as within 24 hours I received a phone call to say that I had got the job and they wanted to take up references. I was thrilled, and a bit daunted, getting the job was one thing, doing it was quite another.

I had learned a great deal during my five years in Tower Hamlets. I had a reasonable level of both confidence and competence, I thought, but it was in a reasonably safe environment that I had created for myself.

Many of my colleagues at the start of my social work career had doubts as to whether I would cope. How would I find my way to the clients' homes? How would I cope with the paperwork? There were no computers in the mid 1970's, but having been a typist I was probably better placed than most to produce the case records and court reports required, than many of my colleagues. I had, in the five years I worked there, managed to overcome most of their prejudices and doubts. I had probably the biggest caseload of all the social workers and had been promoted to the highest grade of social worker then in existence, short of management. I had qualified as an approved Mental Health Officer (which was extremely rare for a blind person to achieve), and I had successfully managed a team of social workers, admittedly only for a few months. I loved the direct contact with the young people and enjoyed taking them for outings to the theatre, zoo, museums or cafés, to give them a range of normal experiences which, in care, they would not otherwise have experienced.

I had however been doing the work for over five years and was becoming increasingly annoyed at how I, and my colleagues, were managed. I thought, probably somewhat arrogantly, that I could do it better, but could I? It would mean leaving my nicely developed comfort zone, but I was ready I thought for another challenge. This need for new challenges would become a recurring theme for the next 30 years!

I had started to ski competitively at the first Paralympic Winter Games in 1976 and at the time of the showing of "This is Your Life" in January 1982, I had performed fairly well at the second Winter Paralympics in Norway in 1980. I was by then preparing for the first World Championships to be held in Switzerland in March 1982. Was this really the best time to be considering a career move? I had been confident in the interview that I could do the job in the assessment unit, but could I?

Chapter 3

Onwards and Upwards

1982

Despite my doubts and experience at the interview, I was still more than a little surprised when I got the job at the new regional assessment centre in Hackney. On the one hand it was a sense of going home i.e. working back in Hackney only a few hundred yards from where I had my accident and had lost my sight. On the other hand, I was ready for a new challenge and this new job would certainly provide it! So I decided to go for it. Once I had the formal written offer of the job I gave in my notice. I was then somewhat overwhelmed by the warmth of the sentiments displayed towards me. Colleagues were genuinely pleased for me and yet sad to be losing a colleague that they actually seemed to value.

The offices in which I worked were an old children's home and had a large room at the back. There had been some memorable parties or leaving do's, and I wanted mine to be one of the best, if not "the best". I arranged for a 9 gallon barrel of beer to be delivered and invited all my colleagues to join me, and somewhat surprisingly, they all turned up.

The party was in many ways the easy bit, but saying goodbye to the kids was very emotional. Many of the kids I was working with had been abandoned by their parents, brutalised or abused by adults in their lives, had no responsible adult to look after their interests or guide them in the right direction, or simply care for them. There was a lot of so called professionalism discussions re getting too close to your "clients", and a lot of soul searching as to whether you could do the job well if you either cared too much or too little. Nowadays I suspect that social workers wouldn't have the time, or permission, to take children to places like the Chislehurst Caves or the London Dungeons, but I had done that regularly in the summer as part of my establishing links to the young people or children in my care. Would they see my leaving them as yet another abandonment?

By the summer of 1982 therefore, I had competed very successfully in the first Winter World Skiing Championships for the disabled, had said my goodbyes, and was ready to face the challenges of working in residential care. I had, when training, had a placement in a children's home in Camden, but I was soon to find out that it was a totally different ball game to the assessment centre at which I was now a first tier manager.

My first day at the assessment centre started with a difficult journey to get there which tested my mobility skills to the full. I used, in those days, a long cane and the journey into central London's Liverpool Street station was not too bad. It involved walking to the station (about half a mile) and then taking the District Line to Mile End and a quick hop across the platform to get the Central Line to Liverpool Street. Fairly easy and a journey I had done in the past. The first big problem was trying to circumnavigate the mainline station and find the right platform, which was not always the same each day. As I was going out of London in the rush hour the train was amazingly empty, and I then had to worry about not only getting off at the right stop, but getting off on the right side of the train, as there was nobody else in my carriage and of course there were no on train announcements in those days. Hackney Station, when I got there, was a typical run down east London station with nobody around to show me which end of the platform the exit was, or whether it was steps down or up to the exit.

Once I got out of the station, I followed the directions I had been given which led me under the railway arches and across the forecourts of seemingly hundreds of impromptu car repair garages. I felt a bit like Tommy, the pinball wizard as I bounced from car to car and eventually arrived at the unit. My problems didn't end there though, as I couldn't find the doorbell or any other means of letting them know I had arrived!

I eventually got let in when someone else arrived for work, not the start I would have hoped for. I could just imagine the staff chatting:

"What do you think of the new manager?

And the reply:

"If he can't even find his way into the building - well!"

The unit had not started taking residents and we were told that we had a few weeks of induction and training before the unit actually opened for business. I met all the other senior staff and they all seemed great, if a bit cautious about me and my disability. I then had to familiarise myself with the layout of the building. I was reluctant to use my cane indoors as this was not something I usually did, but swallowed my pride and used it for the first 2 days to ensure that I indeed did know the layout of the units, and would feel confident to walk around using my hearing and general orientation skills. I then met the staff I would be supervising. There were about 8 care staff and 2 night staff who I would be responsible for. I had my own office which doubled up for the staff room, but soon established that I wanted staff out in the unit and not using the office as a retreat.

The first day of the proper induction did nothing to allay my fears. We covered in some detail the likely violence from the girls and learned holding techniques which later got referred to as "pin down" restraint.

I must admit that for me the holding technique did impose a level of control over the girls, and for many of them, it was the first time they had been held by a man without a sexual component involved. The technique involved getting behind the girl that was kicking off, putting your arms around her, and then sitting on the floor bringing the girl down between your legs which you then placed over her legs to stop you being kicked to death. You then held the girl until she calmed down talking to her gently whilst you held her firmly. Easier said, than done. I did have occasion to use the technique a few times and I must admit the girls seemed to acknowledge that possibly for the first time in their lives, an adult was taking physical control of them, and used it as a safe environment to vent their frustration and rage.

We also had training a bit similar to that which I had received re mental health. This meant taking basic precautions such as not wearing ties or anything around the neck that could be used to strangle; not wearing jewellery that could be used to mark or disfigure; and to try and ensure that we were never left alone for any length of time with any of the girls. I thought at first, that they regarded me as so boring that they didn't want to inflict me on the girls, but did eventually tumble to the fact that they wanted to protect me from any allegations of impropriety!

During this pre-opening period I also worked on admission procedures, medical screening and examinations, emergency evacuation procedures, fire drills, case recording protocols, and all the plethora of administrative processes that have to be in place for a unit such as the one we were opening.

I did, in addition to all the above, organise a couple of social events to get to know the staff better, and these proved popular and established me from the outset, as a bit of a social animal. We had one blow however to our preparations, which I later came to regard as an enormous blessing. Our secure prison unit had had its licence withdrawn which meant that we would not have any admissions from the outset of girls at the top end of the tariff, such as those awaiting trial for murder or serious assault. The reason for the licence being withheld was that a girl had hanged herself in another secure unit on a window catch, which was the same window design as had been installed in our unit.

After about eight weeks training we were as ready as we were ever likely to be. I had a good staff group that I had built a level of trust in, and I think they had rapidly grown to trust me. We had all the furniture in place (mainly beanbags for the girls to sit on as they didn't hurt as much when they threw them at you!). We had a rough idea what we were in for, and although the training and issues outlined above scared the shit out of me, we were ready. All we now needed was the girls!

Chapter 4

My Gals

1982-84

Working with the girls proved to be every bit as challenging as I had expected and more! Some of the girls used my disability as a weapon and others seemed to let their hard exterior image drop, and I saw compassion and genuine care displayed. It was not all bad, with some amusing times, and I really did get to know some of the girls at a deeper level than I would have experienced undertaking field social work.

Working in the unit certainly was a shock. I saw damaged girls whose parents I would cheerfully have strangled (not a social work attitude I know) but you could clearly see the lack of love and parenting at the root of the girls problems. I had to deal with pregnancy terminations, victims of rape, prostitution, and youngsters who were so out of control and lacking in boundaries, they were significantly vulnerable and at risk.

I learned a great deal about myself too. Dealing with aggression, both verbal and physical, helped build my self-confidence. I learned different coping mechanisms to deal with different situations and individuals, and developed and used my other senses to assess situations.

I also posed a dual challenge to the girls - I was a male authority figure and was also disabled. Many of the girls did not know how to treat me i.e. with the usual aggression to authority and to men, or with some kind of benevolence usually shown to the "less fortunate and disabled"!

Sometimes my disability was used by the girls to try and get under my skin or professional guard; other times I used it unashamedly to try and connect to a girl at some different level than they were used to. The use of my disability as a weapon by the girls was something I had not really experienced, and initially I found it difficult and was uncertain how to react. When an out of control 15 year old is shouting and screaming at you and calling you all the "blind ..." under the sun, it is a bit difficult not to take it personally as the only "blind ..." in the room!

It was not all drama and firefighting however and there were many moments of humour and real engagement with the girls.

I remember a conversation with a 14 year old Cypriot girl who had behavioural problems but also moderate learning difficulties. She was in the unit largely for her own safety as she was regarded as extremely vulnerable to sexual exploitation. On one occasion she absconded whilst on a trip to the local park. When she was eventually returned it appeared from the Police and from the girl herself, that she had been seen going off in the park with a man. I, together with a female member of staff, was trying to ascertain whether she had been raped or had had sex with the man. I, during my interview with her, was trying to use words that she might understand. I thought that asking her if she had had intercourse would not be appropriate, and asking her if she had had sex would not do either as sometimes "sex" in some cultures could mean just kissing. I eventually asked her, "When you were in the park and went off with the man, err how far did you go?"

I thought this was a very good non-leading question, designed to ascertain whether she and the scumbag had had sex. The girl then answered me truthfully and immediately, she said "Right behind the bushes."!!

Despite the seriousness of the situation my colleague and I could barely stop ourselves from laughing.

On the other side of the coin, so to speak, was a challenging interview I undertook with the deaf parents of a girl who had been admitted, who had self-harmed. She was depressed and was involved in criminal and anti-social behaviour. The girl had normal hearing which made her a bit of an outcast in her family (the parents were profoundly deaf, both had siblings who were deaf and I think they had another child who was also deaf). British Sign Language (BSL) was their means of communication so I had to visit with an interpreter and it felt somewhat surreal for a social worker with a disability, to be discussing with parents with a disability, the effects of their disability on their daughter, who did not have a disability. Well you get my drift.

On another occasion, I had been called to deal with an incident in the education unit, just as I was going to sit down to lunch. I put my lunch in the oven to keep warm, dealt with the incident, and then returned to the unit on my own to resume my lunch. It was lovely and peaceful after the violent incident I had just been handling and I was relishing the peace and quiet. I sat down and was tucking into my pork chop and veg when I experienced the closest thing to an hallucinatory episode I had ever had. As I lifted the pork chop towards my mouth, it was pulled away from me as if by another force or being.

I was more than a little frightened – was it a poltergeist, or the result of too much alcohol the night before? I was alone in the unit with forces I could not comprehend. With more than a little trepidation I somewhat shakily asked "Is there anyone there?". I reached my hand out to the other side of the chop. I was then gripped with a multitude of emotions: relief, shame at my stupidity, and anger. The external force, or being, in the room was the Unit's bloody cat which had its teeth firmly embedded in my chop!

The chop, and the cat flew through the room and thankfully he never came near me again after that.

I was unsure why some of the girls were in the unit. One girl was certainly not aggressive and out of control. I was fairly certain she was clinically depressed which, at the age of 13, was particularly concerning. She was always miserable and sad and had the unfortunate name of Happiness!

Another memorable moment came towards the end of my work at the centre. For reasons I will go into later, the unit was going through a very difficult time and was due to be closed down. The uncertainty of the future really unsettled the girls who, whilst not wanting to be in the unit, knew where they were and what the rules were, which was a strange comfort for some of them.

I worked a basic shift pattern in the unit which involved an afternoon shift, followed by a sleep-over (where you were an extra pair of hands if things went wrong), and then an early shift. I went into the unit one Tuesday and was immediately aware of the tense atmosphere there. A couple of staff on the shift had reported in sick (possibly as a response to the tensions and threat of violence in the air). The afternoon shift passed fairly uneventfully and I went to bed at about 11pm after supervising the night staff. At around 1 am it all kicked off, with girls fighting, being aggressive to the staff, trying to barricade themselves into their rooms, and it was all hands on deck to calm things down. By the time the next shift were due to clock on the following day the outgoing staff were exhausted, but the girls seemed to have got their second wind and kicked off again!

A few of the staff offered to stay on, but as the senior manager I had no choice but to remain and supervise. The next 24 hours were a repeat of the previous 24, with lulls in the acting out and then upsurges of violence and destruction. Things eventually calmed down on the Thursday evening and I left the unit on the Friday morning exhausted. It is amazing that, at times of crisis it is the strangest and funniest things you remember.

When I went to work on that Tuesday I had not taken a change of clothes or underwear with me. Faced with the aggression and violence over the 3 days, believe me I needed to change my underwear. We had a small store of basic girls' clothing to respond to emergency admissions. In the store were packs of girl's paper knickers which were made to look a bit girly with paper frills around the gussets. I took a pair of the largest knickers and was wearing them on the way home, and remember thinking: "Oh God, please don't let me have an accident now as I would have a bit of explaining to do!"

During my time at the unit, I was also in intensive training for my skiing events, the most significant of which was the 3rd Winter Paralympics to be held in Austria in 1984. The shift work at the unit played havoc with my training regime but one advantage of our prison unit not being licensed was that the enclosed exercise yard was totally unused. It had a high wall all around it and measured about 30 metres square. I used to go out there when off duty and run around the perimeter trailing my hand along the wall and then using my hearing to locate when I was getting to the opposite wall. I remember being greeted by a member of staff when I came in from a training session once, who said that the unit had had a phone call from someone overlooking the building to say that someone was trapped in the yard and was running round and round like a lunatic trying to get out!

Although there were odd incidents which brought a smile to my face, there were many situations which were emotionally draining, or challenged one's beliefs or personal code. One such case was Chrissie who was a tall, intelligent, articulate, verbally aggressive 15 year old. She had been admitted to the assessment unit because of her aggressive behaviour and was thought to be out of control. She demanded answers to everything that you were doing and I remember many arguments and discussions re policies, and her challenging every decision you made. Beneath this brash aggressive young woman, was someone desperate to be loved and shown affection. She, more than any of the other girls, used my disability as a weapon, taunting me that I couldn't see what she was up to, and often challenged me as to how someone who is blind could be in charge.

She got picked up and "befriended" by the ticket clerk at the local railway station, in her search for affection I believe, and ended up pregnant. Our psychologist and Chrissie's mother met with her, and reached the decision that she should have an abortion. Staff had to support Chrissie irrespective of whether they agreed with the decision or not, which, for some, was extremely difficult. I remember going into the local hospital after Chrissie had had the abortion and instead of the angry, abusive argumentative teenager I was greeted affectionately by a frightened little girl!

As if the unit didn't have enough problems dealing with the girls' issues, there developed a major issue with the behaviour of a couple of the senior staff members. One of the managers seemed to be able to do and say what he wanted and the Principal did nothing to correct him. Whilst on a training course, the manager in question openly had sex with a junior member of staff in the men's dormitory, where all the male staff, including the Principal, were staying. One of these staff members, whom I supervised, made a formal complaint. The Principal said he was not aware of anything going on, even though he was in the room, and that the staff member must have made it up. The complainant was my member of staff so I was left to manage the issues raised.

The Principal also had a young girl staying with him who had been a resident of his previous children's home. The Principal insisted that his relationship was on a "father/daughter" basis but nobody believed it. The behaviour of the Manager got worse and he, plus the Principal, were eventually suspended pending investigation.

The Head of Care, who had worked with both of the suspended staff previously, and was effectively the unit Deputy, resigned and left at the same time as the suspensions. It was decided that the unit would close, partly as a result of the senior staff investigations, and partly because it had been confirmed that the unit would not be licensed as a secure unit, as the necessary significant money would not be spent to change the windows and their locks. I got promoted to Acting Head of Care to work with the Head of Education to calm things down, find new placements for all the girls and see what I could do to support and link staff into new jobs.

I mentioned earlier that I had started to seek new challenges, but this experience almost finished me and certainly made me doubt myself rather than increase my confidence.

As a senior manager, I felt responsible for the demise of the unit. Should I have been more aware as to what was going on?

Despite the chaos and incidents, the unit did manage to do some exceptional work with very disturbed and out of control girls. All of that now was destroyed and the girls were all due for yet another change and another regime.

The last few weeks were fraught to say the least. We had journalists camped out on the balconies of the flats opposite trying to get pictures of our girls. Of course "my gals" obliged by stripping off and posing half naked at their windows.

One night we had a mini riot with a number of the girls very determined to go to an all-night party and with us equally determined that they would not. In desperation I gave instructions for the girls' outdoor clothes to be taken away - that would stop them farting in church I thought. Not a bit of it, they just went in their nighties!!

I remember some of the headlines in the Hackney Gazette. There was speculation as to what the centre was going to be turned into and the headline read: "Teenage brothel to be turned into old people's home"!

Within days we had dozens of applications from dirty old men.

Some of the girls were discharged home, too soon in my opinion, but given the closure of the unit it was thought to be expedient. I came across one of the girls from the unit in my next job, and I was convinced that, the closure of the unit hastened her further decline and eventual involvement in mainstream prostitution and drug taking.

Adel was only 12 when she came into the unit. She presented as very much a "Lolita" figure. She was sexually active and we suspected that her mother had been involved in some way as her pimp. She was fun and very much a little girl on the one hand, but with the experience of someone twice her chronological age. She spoke very babyishly and somewhat coquettishly but had a will of iron. When I met her some 18 months later whilst escorting her from a children's home in Islington to a new secure unit in south London, she pulled a knife on the car driver and myself which I had to remove from her. At the Unit in Hackney she was just regressing back to being a 12 year old girl. When I saw her aged 13 and a half, I felt that she was already beyond reach, but I hope I was wrong. She was using drugs and alcohol, and I think I heard later, that she had been "sprung" from the secure unit by her pimp!

Amidst all this, I had to think about what I was going to do next. The experience at the assessment unit had seriously undermined my self-confidence. Would I be able to get a job in social work again at any level let alone management?

Throughout my time at the assessment unit, I had used my sporting activities as a key outside focus from work. If I am honest, my sporting passions probably preserved my sanity. I had the little matter of the Winter Paralympic Games to compete in during 1984 and I was not going to let all my hard training and fundraising schemes go to waste. I had started to manage the ski team, and had become increasingly aware how much my sports management skills applied to certain situations in the unit. Equally, my unit management skills, especially the use of psychology, were applicable in a sports setting.

Should I consider a job in sport or should I go back to a social work job?

Chapter 5

Sporting Success Gives Me Confidence!

1976-84

My international sporting career had started in 1976 when, as a student at North London Polytechnic, I competed at the first Winter Paralympic Games. As I mentioned in my first book, "Where There's A Will", my love of, and participation in sport, was the main crutch I leaned on to aid my adjustment to being blind.

I had, by 1976, tried over 20 sports most of which I was absolutely useless at. The most important thing though was that I had decided for myself that I was useless, not someone else telling me that blind people couldn't do certain sports. Since going blind at aged ten I had been searching for a sport that I could excel at and that I enjoyed. I had tried running, and was an adequate jogger. I had played five aside football and was a good defender. What I lacked in skill I made up for in brute force. A keen cricketer I had developed skill as a good fielder and stalwart number 10 blocker. Having been a good diver when I could see, I was a reasonable swimmer but not very competitive as my main stroke was backstroke. I had set up the

Metro Sports Club in 1973, the British Ski Club for the Disabled in 1974, but was still looking for that ultimate challenge.

In 1974 I was asked if I would like to get some of my friends to try cross country skiing in Norway. My first reaction was "you must be joking" but adopted the attitude "if the Norwegian blind can do it then so can we". I had a great guide (Guttorm, who later appeared as a guest on my "This Is Your Life") and I fell in love with the sport. Cross country skiing demands the highest level of aerobic fitness of any sport and, at last, I had found a sport that demanded high levels of physical fitness and significant levels of mental agility and ability. The only problem was we didn't have any snow in Britain to train on. I therefore had to travel to Norway frequently to train, what a hardship, but it did cost money which, at that time I didn't have.

The 1976 first Winter Paralympic Games in Sweden saw our team of six skiers (1alpine and 5 cross country) under prepared, under equipped but with masses of spirit and commitment. We also had a television crew filming us at the Games. In those days "This Week" was a major documentary series and thought that it was worth covering the fact that 3 blind skiers from the UK were attempting to compete in skiing!

My involvement in the "This Week" programme did however have unforeseen consequences. My 2 friends and I who were featured on the programme got on very well with the producer and interviewer and spent a lot of time with the administrator/researcher Edna, whose job it was to build up a profile of us for inclusion in the documentary. We had a great time with the film crew that came out to Sweden to film us, and one of them, Nino, even had to break into our accommodation for us as we had been locked out having been taken out for a late night celebratory meal and drink by the TV company. That, as they say, is another story.

Five years later, Edna was a researcher for another ITV programme, "This Is Your Life". Souvenir Press were publicising the publication of "Where There's A Will" and a copy of the book landed on Edna's desk. She immediately recognised me and apparently recounted some of the things we got up to and the profile details she had assembled. This interested the producers and they made contact with Mo to suggest that they might feature me as a subject. When they did eventually collar me for the programme, the front cover of the book then acted as the stage backdrop.

Having competed in the first Winter Paralympics I was determined that, if the chance came again in four years, we would be better prepared, equipped and better trained.

In 1977 I met an amazing guy called Rolf Wilhelmson. I was training in Norway at the annual Beitostølen Ski week and he was allocated to me as a guide. We got chatting and it turned out that Rolf was the Managing

Director of ICI Scandinavia. He was a sports fanatic like me, and by the end of the week skiing together, he had agreed to look at possible sponsorship, to act as an official at my forthcoming first Metro Athletics championships in London, and had offered to recruit some ski racing guides for the team. This friendship and support lasted for the next 20 years, and needless to say, Rolf was one of the guests on "This Is Your Life".

We were also fortunate to be supported by a travel company who helped subsidise our training trips to a ski lodge in Rjuken in Telemark, Norway. We used to train there with the British Marines who were doing their Arctic training. Rolf had come up trumps with finding some top class guides, and the remote centre provided the perfect venue for our training. There was a 2.5 kilometre loop that we could train on by ourselves. Rod, the ski centre owner placed a snow plough at the beginning and end of the course, and we could use our hearing to locate when we were at the end of the course.

I say "hearing" in relation to the ski ploughs because objects cast an audible shadow as well as a light shadow. People born blind have a highly developed sound shadow sense but often don't know what it is. I had developed a fairly acute sound shadow sense since going blind aged 10, but it was not nearly as developed as my ski team mates who had been blind from birth.

So, 1980 saw me and several friends setting off to the second Winter Paralympic Games in Geilo, Norway. I had taken on responsibility for managing the preparation of the team. Via Rolf and a few other fundraising ideas, I had managed to generate enough funds to ensure we had good skis, appropriate clothing and top quality guides. The fact that all our guides came from Norway, was particularly helpful as the Games were in their country.

The training, along with the injection of funding for our equipment etc., paid off and we had our first top ten finishes. The progress we had made, and our commitment, struck a chord with Rolf and he undertook to support us even more when we said that we wanted to be even better in 1984 at the next Games.

In 1981 I decided to undertake one of my most ambitious sporting projects to date. A sighted friend in England, and a cross country skier himself, asked me if I fancied having a go at one of the main ski marathons. It would be over 42 kilometres and was called the "Engadine" and was in Switzerland. I, of course said yes and off we set in March 1981. The start of the race was very near to our hotel in Silvaplana, and whilst I was a bit nervous on the way to the start, I was quietly confident.

Nothing had prepared me though for a mass start of over 12,000 skiers all trying to get to the best tracks first. I remember annoying my guide John who had got us close to the perfect point to start the race, by announcing that I desperately needed a pee. Luckily I couldn't understand the curses and swearing I provoked as they were in a foreign language when I skied across skis or pushed the odd skier over. These curses were not a patch however on the vitriol I provoked on the way back from relieving myself!!

The first 15 kilometres were on the flat and there were dozens of tracks for the skiers to aim for. After 15k however, the tracks reduced to only 4 tracks just as we started to climb. The course took us up the side of the San Moritz Cresta bobsleigh run and then, of course, down the other side!

One of the most important tactics/skills to get right in cross country skiing, is the type and thickness of wax you place under your skis. Because you have to propel yourself across the flat you want skis that will glide over the snow with the least resistance but enough to enable you to grip as you kick the ski forward. When you climb the hills you lean forward and, pressing down on the fronts of your skis, you sprint up the hill. Coming down you need the longest glide possible to make the best use of the speed for either the next hill or flat area.

I managed to do the climbing bit fairly well, inflicting the least amount of carnage on my fellow competitors, but then came the most rapid and crowded downhill section I had ever experienced.

My guide John and I had managed to devise a cunning signalling system for when we either got separated or it was too noisy for me to hear his voice commands. John had strapped a cowbell to each of his ski sticks with a high note on the left one and a low note on the right. We only hoped that a farmer would not be herding his cows on the day of the race!

As we had made pretty good progress at the 20k stage there were hundreds of skiers around us but literally thousands behind us. The most frightening bit was yet to come. The course wound its way through the countryside and at several points went under road bridges. The organisers had placed layers of snow under the bridges and mattresses and padding on the bridge's sides in case the skiers could not stop. John, if he could get near me, held the top of my stick and provided steerage and an extra point of balance as we hurtled down the mountain.

I remember flying down the hill like Franz Klammer to the sound of frantic cow bells ringing in my ears. At one stage there was a long downhill with a sharp left-hand turn at the bottom straight under a low bridge. I felt a bit out of control and started to freeze and stiffen up when I heard John hysterically screaming "left". I am not sure who was the most surprised, me, or the people whose picnic I destroyed as I veered right off course and plunged through their picnic table, scattering chairs, flasks and food!

There wasn't even any time to stop and say sorry, as I was still travelling at quite a speed and had somehow managed to turn enough left to enter the tunnel under the bridge.

I am not sure what it is about some sporting events, but it seems to bring the worst out of some people and a level of aggression they would be ashamed of in any other circumstances.

When people fell, they were unceremoniously dragged aside to avoid them getting trampled underneath all the skis. As I thrust forward I remember suddenly finding that my left ski was higher than the right one. John then shouted at me that I had, in fact, skied over the back of a female skier who had fallen and that the front of my ski had gone through the strap of her rucksack which was still on her back!! I am totally ashamed now to say that my first thought was not for her welfare, her safety or her possible injuries, but my own selfish needs. I screamed at the woman, "you've ruined the wax on my skis", and wondered whether I would be able to finish the race?

If that woman, should by any chance, ever read this book, I hope she will accept my most profuse apologies for my animal-like behaviour, and I hope the ski shaped welts eventually faded from her back.

It got worse however, when I placed all my weight on my right ski which was also on the poor woman's back, pulled my left ski from under her strap and then leapt off her back and carried on.

Having got through physically unscathed but with a massive dent to my moral code, I carried on but the worst was yet to come. The temperature had dropped significantly the other side of the mountain and I started to slide and slip and fall. I can't really blame the lady on the floor for my sliding and slipping, just insufficient wax for the conditions and my exhaustion. Every time I fell it was more and more difficult to get up. I felt like "a sheep on its back" as, having fallen, I tried to get up with 2 six foot planks on my feet. At one point, semi delirious, I attempted to crawl on all fours! I eventually pulled myself together and plodded on but by that stage I was very nearly at the point of total exhaustion. I had never experienced those levels of physical and mental extremes before and I learned a great deal as to what my body was capable of.

As we came to the finish, we were funnelled into lanes to the finishing line when our electronic number tags would be swiped and our time recorded. My last memory of the race was, somewhat deliriously, plodding forward muttering to myself "left foot, right foot, left foot right foot". I then found my progress halted. I walked forward but couldn't progress and if anything got pushed backwards. John was yelling at me but I was beyond listening or hearing anything at that stage. He eventually came up behind me and grabbing my ski suit pulled me backwards, lined me up, and then shoved me forward. Just as well he did as I could have still been there today. The halt to my progress had been the lane rope and pole between my legs (lucky I wasn't going fast)!

When I was eventually in a state to take in what was happening around me I felt somewhat disappointed at our time. We had completed the first half of the race, which included the long flat section plus most of the steep ups and downs, in2 hours. The second half had taken over 3 hours, but John later admitted that he had been seriously worried about my health, as he thought on more than one occasion that I was going to collapse or pass out.

We also learned that the conditions were some of the worst experienced in the history of the race. This made me feel slightly better, and I managed to put it in perspective in that hundreds had not finished the race at all; we had finished two-thirds down the field in 7291st place, and that we had beaten over 5000 other skiers.

I am sure this experience set me up both physically and mentally for the first World Skiing Championships for the disabled to be held in Switzerland in 1982. I, and the team, performed well, with me achieving my highest individual placing of 7th in the Biathlon (which is a combination of skiing and shooting).

Having changed jobs in 1982 to work in the assessment centre, I was not sure whether I would still be able to both fundraise and train for the next Winter Paralympics to be held in Austria in 1984.

We were aspiring to even greater levels of fitness and preparedness and this would take even more funds, so despite the pressures of work, I embarked on perhaps my maddest period of fundraising and sport up until then.

I can't remember how it came about, but someone, (it might have been me), came up with the wacky idea that the three of us in the ski team (Peter, Jimmy and I), should attempt 3 marathons in 3 different sports in 30 days.

We were all skiers so that was taken for granted to be one of the 3 sports but what others could we do? We all ran as part of our training so we decided that the London Marathon would be the second sport chosen. That just left one more. Jim had been doing some canoeing and had heard of a marathon called "the Devizes to Westminster Canoe race". We all thought, sitting down in a boat can't be that much of a problem, we were fit, and had good upper body strength, so why not?

I had devised a cunning plan whereby we would sell draw tickets, on which, purchasers would write down the combined time they thought it would take me, to do all 3 marathons.

The skiing event we chose was the Holmenkollen Ski Marathon over a distance of 42 Kilometres in Norway. Our guides were all Norwegian and it saved us money flying them to another country. My experience of this marathon was a distinct contrast to the one I had completed in Switzerland in 1981. I was a better skier, I knew a bit what to expect and the conditions were good. I finished it in just over 4 hours and was somewhat elated and flattered when, as I entered the finishing area, they played "God Save the Queen". I thought it was a fantastic feat of organisation whereby they could identify each competitor as they finished and play their national anthem. What I hadn't realised was that what we refer to as our "national anthem" the Norwegians call "The King's Song", and was played every time the King of Norway appeared at a public function. As it happened, just as I was finishing, the King of Norway entered the arena on skis just behind me! Well I am sure you would have thought the same as me!

We were all set then for the second of the marathons, the canoe one, some 2 weeks later. It is here, that I must own up to a serious lack of judgement and research. Having entered the race I then found out that, although it was a marathon, it was over 125 miles! Never having canoed in my life I had to undertake some extensive canoe training, but by the time of the race I had only paddled a maximum of 20 miles in one go. It got worse however, when I was told that there were 72 of something called portages in the race, whereby you had to lift the canoe out of the water and run with it around the lock and put the canoe back in the water and carry on. The longest portage was one and a quarter miles and the 20 foot plus canoe had to be laden with our survival kit.

I should add that I was not alone in the canoe. It was a double one and I had managed to find a guide, Charley, who was even madder than I was, but at least was an experienced canoeist.

We set off, aptly on April Fool's day, from Devizes and paddled our way down the Kennet and Avon canal. We had arranged for 2 support crews to act as our backup, providing us with changes of clothing, hot drinks and sports drinks through the night.

I looked very elegant in my thick ladies tights, hockey boots and t-shirt. The first portage didn't occur for about 30 miles into the race, and if we kept our five miles an hour paddling pace up we should arrive there in about six hours. The night before we set off, I thought to ask my guide "what happens when you need a wee?" Charley, unphased said, "you just pee yourself in the boat!" I thought "how disgusting", I couldn't do that, and I shuddered to think what the answer would have been if I wanted to "do number two's"!

As we paddled hour after hour I felt the growing need to pee and after about five hours I did as Charley had predicted, pee myself in the boat. It was a cold day and so I had mixed feelings of relief, gratifyingly pleasant warmth, and disgust as I sat there in my own pee.

We then after six hours of paddling got to the first portage. We had trained for this moment, so we leapt out of the boat, put the paddles inside, hoisted the boat over our heads, and started running. My relief of being out of the boat after six hours paddling, and the elation of being able to stretch my legs as we ran, was soon obliterated by the realisation of what was trickling down over me from the boat above my head!

We paddled through the night in some of the worst conditions in the history of the race. We had sleet and hail stones, almost hit a barge when Charley fell asleep, and were nearly capsized on the final leg on the Thames, by the river police. The canoe race was timed to finish on the morning of the boat race and the police were clearing the rowing course of driftwood and rubbish. We eventually climbed out of the boat on the small stretch of beach by Westminster Bridge. As you can imagine we stank! We had taken just over 27 hours non-stop and Charley, my fantastic guide, passed out as we walked onto the bridge. Of the 182 crews that had started the race, only 82 had finished, and we were 41st overall, I think it was the biggest achievement of my life and the exhaustion I felt was very similar to my hazy memory of the Engadine ski marathon 2 years earlier. Whilst this canoe marathon I think is my greatest sporting achievement, I have never been in a canoe since. For 27 hours all I had to focus on was my need to get to Westminster. My fingers were curved permanently in the shape of the paddle, I was unable to stand unaided, and I had lost about seven pound in weight during the race. Apparently, I looked so ill when I finished, that Mo, who had gone to Westminster Bridge to meet me, burst into tears as she thought I was dying.

I had real doubts that I would be fit enough to run the London Marathon 2 weeks later, and the thought, that I would need to keep as my goal Westminster Bridge again, (the finishing post of the London Marathon in those days), gave me the shudders and evoked the worst memories from the canoeing.

Some intensive physio, lots of hot baths, and virtually 2 weeks total rest, went some way to restore me and I lined up with yet another great guide, Les, to start the London Marathon. I was not aiming for a time and just wanted to finish. By the time of the last of the three marathons, I had sold over £3000 worth of tickets but needed to complete them all to get an overall time, so no pressure then.

My guide was used to running at 7 minute mile pace and on his advice, we took on water at every drinks station from the start. We obviously didn't sweat at my more sedate 12 minute mile pace, and by the time we had done

12 miles my guide was busting for a pee. I had been struggling from about six miles and the thought that I still had 20 miles to go filled me with dread. I was also seizing up badly and thought "if I stop whilst Les goes to the toilet I won't be able to get going again". Les couldn't hold on and I suffered the ignominy of being parked at the side of the road, with Les asking a spectator to look after me like a stray dog, and me running on the spot like a wind-up doll, whilst he relieved himself in a nearby toilet.

The last few miles were agony, with me walking virtually the last six miles. We finished however in five and a half hours; now all three marathons had been completed, and I could legitimately draw down the funds raised.

I also remember saying to myself, "that's it, no more hair brained schemes to raise money just stick to the competitions now".

The old brain does play tricks on us from time to time, and I had completely forgotten these thoughts in 2012 when, again to raise money for charity, I undertook to complete 10 sports in ten months to raise ten thousand pounds, but more of that later.

The three marathons were undertaken during a comparatively calm time at the assessment unit. Which was more than could be said for when I ran the London Marathon again in 1984, and led our team at the third Winter Paralympics in Austria. After my disastrous run the previous year, I was determined to run a marathon with no fundraising pressures and when I was reasonably fit.

With another fabulous guide, John, I completed the 1984 marathon in just over 4 hours. I had a good run and hit the 20 mile mark in 2 hours fifty-three minutes and was hoping for a good time. I then hit the notorious "wall "and completed the last six plus miles in just over 90 minutes. I was pretty fit from having competed in the Winter Paralympics a month earlier. Having had such a good run I decided that I would not run any more marathons as I wanted my lasting memory to be one of enjoyment and success rather than discomfort and agony.

I was on a successful roll in that I and the team had performed very well at the Winter Paralympics; Peter, our top skier, won a bronze medal in the 5k sprint race, and the relay team had finished 5th. I was managing the cross country team as well as competing, and, experienced one of my most treasured sporting memories at these Games.

Peter was on top form but, unusually for him, was having a crisis of confidence. I had to use all of my psychology training to boost his self-confidence. I went through the course with him in his mind i.e. mental mapping, got him to believe that he was the fittest skier in the race (which he probably was), and convinced him that his technique had improved significantly since the last Games (which it probably had not).

The sprint was not his best event as he favoured the longer distances, but I was ecstatic when he came in third. As he stood on the medal podium, the tears flowed down my cheeks. In 8 years we had come from a position of being "no hopers" to being elite skiers and had won a skiing medal. The elation of the Games and the London Marathon success, were soon tempered by my return to work at the assessment centre which was going through its last gasps of life.

Chapter 6

When the Going Gets Tough, the Tough Get Going!

1984

As the Winter Paralympic Games faded from my memory and the work situation got worse, I had to reach a decision as to what I should do next, career-wise. Although I had successfully managed the ski team, I didn't think that I stood any chance of obtaining a job in sports management, and I still had real doubts as to whether I was fit to manage in a new social work setting. I doubted whether I could go back to being a basic grade social worker and anyway, would anyone employ me?

Rather than sending me on gardening leave when the unit closed, they asked if I would like to work temporarily in another setting within the social services department. As a Hackney employee I was eligible for redeployment to a job of a similar grade and for which I had the requisite qualifications and skills. I learned that I had been slotted into a soon to be vacant, fieldwork Team Manager post, but had to decide what to do in the intervening six weeks.

I plumped to work in a nursery and had one of the most fantastic times in my social work career. I worked in the baby unit and changed nappies with the best of them. In those days it was the thick terry towelling nappies which were easier to cope with for us novices. Not having children myself it was all new to me. I experienced all the joys of baby care such as being covered in wee when the winkle of the little boy I was changing, shot up and sprayed me, and the rest of the room! I am sure he would have been a champion piddler in later life and would have no difficulty in getting his wee high up the wall in the toilet if his early performance was anything to judge by!

I played with the older children and was struck at their reaction to me. I was the only male in the unit and many of the children were from single parent families, with limited, if any, contact with their fathers. I played physical games with them and gave them "swing boats" (whereby a child would hold each of my hands and I would then swing them round with them flying outwards in the air).

I am sure health and safety would have something to say about this nowadays but I and the children loved it. I did get warned by the supervisor to calm down as she was worried that the female staff would not be able to play the same games when I left. I had a great time there and it was with a great deal of sadness, and not a little trepidation, that I took up the fieldwork manager post in the Clapton Square office.

My sadness was nothing to do with my new colleagues but more to do with the fact that I had needed the break from the stresses of social work and I was now back coping with the day to day realities and problems that the job threw up. It was, however, a bit like riding a bike, something you don't forget. It was also the best thing, as it happens, that could have happened to me at that stage. I managed to win over the trust of the team members, some of whom were a bit resentful as they had hoped to have applied for the Manager post if it had become vacant. I contributed to the management team meetings, and I regained my confidence and belief in my ability to in fact - manage. So much so, that, after a few months, I decided to apply for an Area Manager's post in the neighbouring borough of Islington.

Some people thought that I had "more front than Brighton" in applying for a promotion so soon after the assessment centre debacle, but I felt I needed to get a job that I had achieved on merit and not been slotted into.

The job I applied for involved managing a small area team with 3 team managers and about 25 social workers. It was in the Essex Road office, which had gained a bit of a reputation in the social work world as being a bit left wing and at one time reputed to be run as "a collective"!

Again, I was surprised when I was shortlisted, and as before set about preparing myself for the interview. It was a strange affair and was as equal opportunity based as the Hackney interview had been prejudicial and biased. Virtually the whole office were involved in one way or the other in the interview process. I spent time with different small groups including the administrators, social workers managers and volunteers. I think I was not what they were expecting and I learned afterwards that they actually had a vote of the whole office as to who should be appointed. I apparently won the vote and I got the call from the outgoing Area Manager to say they would like to offer me the job.

Given this was 1984 the Essex Road office was way ahead of its time re office practices. No staff other than the administrators had personal desks and everyone, including the Area Manager, hot-desked!

Each member of staff had a pigeon hole to keep post or files in. Because I used audio equipment or had things read to me, I said that I would need an office. They acknowledged this practical need and said they would see what they could do. When I arrived on my first day I was shown to my office which was literally a converted cupboard with a window. The room was as wide as the desk and you couldn't open the door if someone was sitting at the desk. I felt touched that they had given my request so much thought but only realised 3 weeks later that there was no light in the room. Initially I wondered if they thought that as I was blind I didn't need one but was told that, as the room had been used as a store room there had been no need for a light. They arranged for one to be installed and then I was up, and running.

Chapter 7

Islington: A Very Different Experience
1984-89

Islington was just the new challenge I needed. I managed different services than I was used to. I learned a great deal. And, oh yes, had a great deal of fun! I enjoyed every minute of my time in Islington. I wanted to keep my practice levels up, so continued operating as an approved Mental Health Officer. This was a bit unusual, as senior managers rarely continued to work in the field, but my hands on approach, fitted in well with the team's ethos.

There were many new challenges as I was now managing children's services, adults' services, including home helps, and a wide range of voluntary groups, including one for people experiencing bereavement and another for those living in isolation.

I recruited a reader to help me with the printed material and we spent many a happy hour wedged in my converted cupboard. The building we were in was over 100 years old and was falling down. The safe had to be placed in the fireplace opening as an earlier attempt to install a safe ended in disaster with it falling through the floor to the room below.

We had to be relocated on 2 occasions - once because of the state of repair and once because of a fire in the main switchboard/post room. We believe it was started deliberately by some intruders (possibly disgruntled clients), and the only real damage done was that the pigeon holes, which all staff used for their post and paperwork, were incinerated.

The fire did come in handy however, as for years to come, every time the office couldn't find a file which we had obviously lost, it was blamed on the fire. I estimate that the fire was reputed to have destroyed enough paper to fill a large house! After the second relocation, it was obvious that the long term use of the building as a public building was both untenable and unsafe. The Council announced a programme of decentralisation and plans were set to open 10 neighbourhood offices. These would house, environmental health, social and housing services. Organising repairs to the old office, and setting up a new office, added a new sphere of management to my portfolio, that of property management.

I also continued my role as the office social secretary and organised many social events for the staff. This was an extremely effective way of gaining trust, building up a team culture, having fun and meeting people in a different context. One of the events I organised however still makes me shudder to this day. Not because it was a bad event, but, it was arranged on the riverboat "The Marchioness", a week after, and at exactly the same time, as the boat sank on the Thames with the tragic loss of so many lives. I don't necessarily believe in fate, but someone was certainly smiling on us at that time. We did continue with a boat disco on another boat, but it was a bit of a subdued event.

I was working in Islington for six years, and was able, throughout my time there, to both undertake direct work with individuals and to manage the office. I ran groups for the home helps, met regularly with a forum for foster parents, and dealt with children in care on a day to day basis.

I also had responsibility for managing a service area that was totally unfamiliar to me, that of severely learning disabled young adults in a residential setting.

I undertook mental health assessments and one in particular, sticks out in my mind. We had been called by the husband of a woman with recurring mental illness episodes. She was extremely agitated and was tearing up paper and clothing. When I and a colleague arrived her husband and her children were sitting frightened and anxious in the kitchen. The woman kept going to the windows and saying that voices were telling her that she should jump out of the fourth floor window and join Jesus.

We completed our part of the assessment and then awaited the arrival of the approved doctor to complete the health component of the Sectioning procedure. He duly arrived and agreed with our assessment that she needed to be admitted to hospital. He signed the paperwork and contacted the ambulance service to be told that there was an ambulance driver strike and that it could take 2 hours to reach us! The doctor left and we sat with the family and the increasingly agitated woman, but we were extremely concerned that she would do something to hurt herself. We chased up the emergency services but were told that they still couldn't say how long it would take.

In the end we decided that we would not wait any longer and I called a minicab to transport her to the hospital. I had booked a bed so they had been expecting us for over 2 hours. When the cab arrived, the woman's husband and I between us escorted her into the cab. The cab driver was very unhappy at taking "a mad woman" in his cab and kept asking us, "she's not going to be sick is she?"

When we arrived at the hospital the woman refused to get out of the cab. We reasoned with her, tried to induce her with the thought of food or peace and quiet, but nothing worked.

I rang the ward to seek assistance, but they said they couldn't help as they were short staffed and were serving supper!

The driver was getting more and more hysterical, so much so, that he said we didn't need to pay and could settle up later if we would only get the woman out of his car.

There seemed to be nothing for it, I gave my bag and white stick to my colleague, came around the car, reached in and picked the woman up bodily and, under the direction of my colleague, carried the woman into the hospital, into the lift and then onto the ward. I thought whatever happens I must not drop her. Imagine the headlines, "blind social worker drops mental health patient in hospital incident".

I spoke to the Charge Nurse later and he said how surprised he was when the lifts opened, and I staggered out with a woman in my arms saying, "Okay, where do you want her?"

Whilst in Islington I had started also to use a very primitive form of computer especially designed for the blind. This enabled me to feel more in control of producing written reports and information. Up until then, I had used a typewriter with someone reading back my typing and correcting it for me. For the first time in my life (since losing my sight) I could produce written material which I could read myself before I submitted it. I could produce print almost anywhere once I had set my machine up and then print it via a very basic dot matrix printer. This may sound pretty crude and basic now, but in the late 1980's it was revolutionary and tremendously empowering.

All the offices in the Islington new building were open plan and I didn't even have a cupboard to call my own. It did mean however that you could hear everything that was going on. Sometimes this caused a distraction and other times, it meant that you were able to intervene if someone was becoming difficult or aggressive. I remember being on duty one day and heard the receptionist trying to deal with a man who was complaining about his housing allocation. The discussion was getting more and more noisy and then I heard the receptionist say,

"Oh God, what are you doing"?

I immediately rushed over to assist and found that the man had superglued himself to the reception desk. It really does dry as quickly as the advert says. I tried to lever him off the desk but he was stuck fast. When the police arrived they didn't have any more success than I did, in unsticking him. In the end, the police undid the man's trousers, slid him out of them, and carted him off. It took us quite a few days, and pints of solvent to get his trousers off the desk. We remained open throughout, and despite having hundreds of people through the door, not a single person asked why we had a pair of men's trousers stuck to our reception desk!

I had continued my ski racing activities during my time in Islington. I was managing the ski team and still fundraising, but no crazy schemes this time. I had started after dinner speaking as a way of raising funds and this proved both enjoyable and immensely profitable.

I raced in the second World Championships in Sweden in 1986, and then the fourth Winter Paralympic Games, which were again held in Austria.

In 1987 I suffered my first really serious sporting injury and was still suffering from its after effects at the 1988 Games. I really should not have gone but the thought of competing had certainly spurred me on to train and do the physio exercises to overcome the injury. The injury occurred when I was skiing in Beitostolen in Norway at the annual ski week, and I decided to have a bit of recreational skiing and try downhill. I did a couple of runs and loved it and seriously considered whether this might be a sport I could do when I retired from cross country racing. I got to the bottom of the run and stopped to talk to some other skiers. I was a bit unsteady on my skis and went to turn my knee sideways and rest it on the snow. Cross country boots are like running shoes and provide the maximum of flexibility; downhill boots are like metal wellingtons on your feet and provide no flexibility what-so-ever. Apparently you could hear the noise of my cruciate ligament rupturing half way up the mountain.

I went to a local treatment centre and they advised me to go to hospital when I arrived back in Britain. I had the leg strapped but couldn't walk on it so spent the last 3 days in bed and had to be wheeled down to the coach to go home, and then had the indignity of being loaded onto the plane in a special chair which felt more like being pushed up a slope in a wheel barrow. At home I was admitted to hospital and the leg put in plaster, I had "only ruptured it" rather than snapped it which apparently was good. I was 38 in 1988 so wasn't sure how many competitive games I had left in me.

I was not the most popular person when I eventually returned to work. I was so bored after a few days of sitting at home in plaster, that I persuaded work to let me travel in via minicab which they would pay for. I had crutches and the leg was plastered from just above the ankle to the top of my thigh. I travelled to and from work by cab for about a month until I eventually had the plaster removed and had the confidence to go back to using public transport.

Every difficult situation I find myself in also seems to provide me with some of my funniest moments. Soon after I was plastered, I was booked to do an important after dinner speech at a Rotary District conference in the Midlands. The booking had been in the diary for months and I didn't want to disappoint them. I worked out that if my friend picked me up from home he could drive me up to the station. Then with my two crutches and my white stick I could be helped through the barriers on to the tube station and be guided down to the platform by the station staff. I could then change tubes by staying on the same platform at the interchange point and pick up the correct tube line which would take me to the mainline station. There, station staff would meet me and with the use of a wheelchair would get me up to the mainline station and onto the train. No problems.

I then spoke to the Rotarian who had been tasked to meet me and host me at the event. He came over as very nervous at hosting a person with a disability, and was even more concerned when I told him that I had had an accident and was in plaster. I went through my planned route and said that with my two crutches, white stick and my leg in plaster I should be pretty safe and would still come. I couldn't believe it when my Rotarian host then asked:

"How will I recognise you?"

After nearly six years in Islington I felt ready for an even greater managerial challenge. I had gained a mass of varied management experience, was fairly competent now in producing printed material, could skim read information quicker than most, and had restored my confidence in my own ability.

I felt I needed to improve my management qualifications and enrolled in a Diploma in Management course whilst in Islington but didn't complete it. I decided, after starting the course, that perhaps yet another challenge awaited me, so I applied for a further promotion in the Royal Borough of Kensington and Chelsea.

I applied for, and got, the job in Kensington, despite yet another strange interview (more about that later). My colleagues arranged a fantastic leaving party for me. We had over 100 guests in the office. We had dancing, speeches and many of the foster parents and some of the children in care also came to the early part of the party. I had been getting a lot of flak from my colleagues that I was going to an area where all the posh people lived. I was ribbed that, as "the boss", I would have to smarten up so I attended my leaving party dressed in my dinner suit and bow tie and said that I had been told that all staff dressed like that in Kensington. The interviewing panel I believed had been wearing formal dress and I asked my guests, as I was blind, whether they thought that I had been lied to?

The joke went down well, and I eventually went home in the early hours considerably the worse for wear. It was a fantastic experience working in Islington and the people were really great. I was, however ready to seek new horizons.

Chapter 8

A Technical Challenge!

1984-2013

I alluded in the previous chapter to the importance of technological innovation in my life. Having been a typist I had good keyboard skills and could also read and write Braille on a manual machine, there being no electronic devices until the late 1980s. I never envisaged however, just how important technology would become in my daily life!

When I wrote my first book "Where There's a Will", in 1980, I typed the whole of the initial draft without being able to read a word. I asked Mo to correct my spelling, make any grammatical changes needed, and then got a neighbour to retype it correcting any typo's and include any alterations made by Mo.

The first time I actually read my own book was when the RNIB put it onto their Talking Book service. The reader is Brian Perkins the ex-news reader. I met him when he was reading the book at the Talking Book Studios and thought he was a bit posh to be reading my story. He did it well however and I will be eternally grateful to the RNIB for using the technology of the day i.e. tape recording and then talking books, to enable me to evaluate and hear my own work.

I am not sure when computers made their appearance in the daily lives of the general population, but in the mid to late 1980's, someone had the fantastic idea that blind people should not be excluded from the technology boom. I had heard from a friend that a machine had been developed which allowed blind people to write non-contracted Braille onto a cassette tape, which could then be processed by the computer and exported to a printer. The machine was called a VersaBraille and I wanted one.

As a senior Manager, I applied to the pre-runner to the current "Access to Work Scheme" for help. This is a Government supported system for providing equipment or financial assistance, to disabled people needing help with either personal or technical support at work. Much of the specialist equipment costs thousands of pounds and would be outside the reach of most people with a disability starting work. I was successful, and I remember my excitement on the day my new equipment arrived. The machine was the size of a small suitcase and that was without the printer. I had to insert a special cassette to enable the machine to operate as a computer and then put another cassette in to input the work on. I can't express just how thrilled I was when I read my own work for the first time on an electronic device. It was by no means portable within the modern understanding of the word, but it was a start. The developers didn't give up however, and soon came the next version called the VersaText. This used the VersaBraille purely as the input device and a small black box as the "computer" which was in turn linked to a printer. The processing and capabilities of the computer were much improved but it was even less portable. The principal however was still one of a specialist device using a Braille keyboard as the means of inputting data.

The VersaBraille machine had a Braille display and the Braille letters were electronically raised by the impulses sent by the computer to tactile pins.

During the early 1990's, significant advances were made and progressed to an inclusive solution, i.e. blind people using the same computer and software as their sighted colleagues. A specialist interface was developed which enabled the blind user to have audible feedback as to what the cursor was pointing to on the monitor screen and also for them to be able to read the letters from the screen on a Braille display. I managed to get the new equipment and benefitted greatly from the inclusion advances.

This meant that I could, for the first time, read anything that someone else had written and therefore, read more easily my staff's and colleagues' reports etc. They could copy their work onto a five and a half inch floppy disk in the early days and later, onto the smaller three and a half inch disks for me to insert into my computer. As an ex typist, I was comfortable using an ordinary qwerty keyboard as it has proved almost impossible for me to use a mouse proficiently. The clever techies however have worked out a key stroke for virtually every action that the mouse performs. The MS-DOS system worked well with the adapted software, as basically the cursor followed the electronic positioning on the screen and therefore on the display. You could, for example, work out how far along a 65 space line of type you were, and visualise the layout of documents.

I got fairly proficient on the computer and having had sight, found I could easily imagine how the document would look and how to move to, and around, different bits of the document on the screen.

The key to the MS-DOS system from a blind person's perspective was its simplicity. Everything my colleagues could see on the screen, especially where the cursor was, I could see on my Braille display or get spoken to me. "Simples" as a well-known meerkat would say.

Then disaster struck, they invented Windows. No not glass things that you look through, but the operating system for computers. This altered the whole of the basis of how to approach working on a computer. Suddenly there could be dozens of icons on the screen and you had to find the one you wanted and select it. The adapted software couldn't do this, and we had to wait some time for the techies to catch up and invent software that could search for icons and select them. It then relied on a range of new techniques within word processing and then email, to interface between the Braille/speech software and the computer.

I started originally to use a specialist access package called Jaws version 4 and now some 20 years later am using version 16. As the Windows platforms have developed, the specialist access packages have had to adapt to meet the new challenges. I am now writing this book using a laptop, with Windows 7 operating system and with Office 10 software. I can print these pages via wifi connectivity to the printer, or copy this onto another computer and print my own Braille copy. I can also copy a word file to my portable book reader and it will read the word document in electronic speech. I now have a scanner linked to my computer, and therefore can read any post that is typed (but no solution has yet been found to reading hand written material). This enables me to have even more independence re handling my own post. I can use virtually every function of the computer from word processing, emails, Access database construction, Excel spread sheets, calendars and contacts.

One of the most inclusive aspects of the technological revolution from my perspective, is the use of electronically produced material either for download or sending via a link. Growing up as someone with sight but then losing it, I always dreamed that one day I would be able to read a daily newspaper again. Most people couldn't envisage how that could ever happen, and I must admit I shared their scepticism. Then about 8 years ago, even this was made possible. I can now receive dozens of daily, weekly or monthly publications direct to my computer. Papers, for example, such as the Daily Telegraph or the Guardian, are sent as an email attachment every day. I can have them as word or html files and I simply open them with a piece of software called the a-technic newsreader, and Bob's your uncle, the paper is there. It mercifully strips out all of the adverts and places all the articles into their respective sub sections such as sport, the city etc. You can also ask for articles containing certain words to be put in a special interests file. I still find this access to the printed word thrilling, and order far too many publications than I can ever hope to read. I just do it because I can!

It is not just computers that have changed my life technology-wise. In the late 1990's the same technology boffins turned their minds to the growing mobile phone explosion. The main problem from a blind person's perspective is that you can't see what is on the screen and therefore cannot use menus, contact lists etc.

This was ingeniously solved by inventing a speech package which audibly spoke the menu item, or the speed dial or the number you are dialling. As the phones developed, so too, did the speech packages and a number of the phone manufacturers included basic speech access as standard in their phones. Orange, one of the main mobile phone service providers, introduced a voice recognition system called "Wildfire". They said that they had to give it a silly name as it had to be a word that could not easily be confused with something else.

I remember using my phone in a public place and being embarrassed to say "hello Wildfire" in case they thought I was talking to one of those sex lines! When connected to Wildfire you just had to ask for the name of the person you wanted to ring and Wildfire then dialled it. Sometimes, Wildfire didn't connect properly and I found myself shouting louder and louder at the phone to make it understand you better - a bit like you do with foreigners who don't understand English. I did feel a bit diffident talking to a phone and remember being astounded one day when Wildfire said,

"I am having difficulty in understanding you, can I just do some checks with you, Please say your name?

I said

"Mike Brace" and Wildfire said

"Thank you I thought so, let me know if anything changes"?

Wildfire then asked:

"Are you male or female?" I of course replied

"Male"

and then Wildfire, with a definite giggle in the electronic voice, said

"I thought so, let me know if anything changes!!!"

This service didn't really take on and it was discontinued some five years ago.

Much like the changes in computing when the Windows operating system was introduced, potential disaster struck in the phone world, (as far as blind users were concerned), when smart phones with touch screens without buttons were introduced. Help though, was just around the corner, in the corporate form of Apple. They had looked at speech on their Apple Mac computers and decided that an inclusive approach should be taken, and incorporated speech and magnification accessibility into all their products. This includes Macs, iPads, iPods and iPhones. With a couple of swipes or with some help from a sighted friend, you can be up and running with your new Apple product "straight out of the box". There is no expensive additional software to download to the phone, and the quality and performance of the speech or magnification is very good.

I can connect my Braille device to my iPhone and my iPad either with a cable or Bluetooth which allows me to read material in Braille and also to input to the devices by my portable Braille keyboard or display.

I now use an iPhone and iPad (as well as my laptop) and can access my address book, send and receive text messages, emails and, of course, receive and make phone calls. I store over 2000 music tracks on the phone and can read daisy books via a book app. There are dozens of other apps you can buy to make life easier. There are accessible apps that can tell you, for example, having logged into the phone, the bus stop where you are waiting, when the next bus no. X is coming! Similarly you can put the station you are waiting at and where you want to go and the phone will check and tell you when the next train is due, and often, which platform it goes from! There are also maps you can access on your phone which provide an auditory commentary via satnav to help you find your way.

One of the most incredible apps though that I have seen and used, is one whereby you can take a picture of an object via the camera on your phone, and send it to a kind of recognition library. If there is an image in the library that matches your upload, then it replies and tells you what it was that you photographed! I also have an OCR application on my mobile phone with which I can take a picture of a printed page, such as a menu or an agenda, and then the phone reads out what was on the paper.

It is not just in the area of high tech that advances have been made though. There are very small portable music or book players. Some include both, plus many other functions. For example, my portable machine which measures about the same size as one of the older mobile phones, enables me to store thousands of tracks in the music section, several books in daisy format, use the alarm and built in clock, and record memos digitally.

Even more widely, there are now talking clocks and watches; talking tape measures; audible spirit levels; liquid level indicators (devices you put either the long or short pins of the gadget, into a cup and when the liquid reaches the pins it bleeps to warn you to stop pouring). I also found by accident, that this device can also be used for testing fuses!

There are machines that allow you to play recordings of the local newspapers via a memory stick, and a fantastic cheap electronic labeller. This gadget, called the PenFriend, comes with hundreds of paper stick on labels that have a small electronic individually numbered bar code within them. When you hold the tip of the electronic pen to the label it bleeps and you begin the recording by speaking into the pen. It then records the information onto the pen but links it to the label's individual number.

Even in my sporting activities technology has helped. In the Biathlon, the shooting aspect was made possible by linking an oscillator to the telescopic sight of the rifle. The target circles are different colours and reflect different levels of light. As you point the gun to the different coloured circles of the target, the note, heard in the earphones, changes, up or down depending on whether you were pointing to the light or dark circles. Once you found the bulls eye and knew whether you were at the top middle, left or right of the circle, you then fired. They have extended this technology to enable blind athletes to undertake archery, shooting and other target related sports.

The difference technology has made to my life, especially in the area of work, has been enormous. I would not have been competitive in many of my jobs, and my horizons have been widened and my knowledge base extended, by being enabled to read a wide selection of books and the broad spectrum of political and journalistic opinion. Who knows what else might be possible in the next 30 years?

Chapter 9

You've got to be Joking!

1977 - 2013

During the late 1970's I started my third career. Alongside my social work and my sport, I began to undertake after dinner speaking to raise awareness of, and challenge prejudice towards, disability. I also managed to raise much needed funding for my various charities.

I started after dinner speaking totally by accident. In the late 1970's I was walking down Marylebone High Street looking for the studios of Radio London when I asked someone for help locating them. A guy took me over the main road and asked me where I was going and why? I explained that I was on my way to do a radio interview re my involvement in sport. He asked if I did talks for other groups and explained that he was involved with a group called "Round Table", which were always looking for speakers to come to their fortnightly meetings. He said he lived in a place called Romford, which, coincidentally, was where I also lived! He asked me if I would come and speak to his "Round Table" and, as I would go anywhere for a free meal and drink, I agreed.

Thus was established my speaking career. At the point of writing I have raised over half a million pounds for my different charities, whilst at the same time challenging peoples' concepts of disability. I talk about "ability" and use humour to make my points and gently poke fun at attitudes and get people to examine what they would do or say in a range of circumstances. I have developed a method of delivering my talks which uses an acronym of a word that might have relevance to the audience. I used, for example, the word "SPORTS" during 2012, which I then went on to unpick letter by letter and recount some of the things that have happened to me, or highlight areas I want to challenge or probe.

After saying a couple of introductory funnies such as "thank you for the introduction; I am always worried how I am going to be introduced, i.e. the introduction goes on for ever and the person introducing you then has said everything you wanted to say in your speech, or it is so brief as to surprise you and you are expected to start before you have got your notes out. The worst introduction however was by someone who himself had a bit of a disability or impediment i.e. he spoonerised everything that he said. He announced one evening that the raffle was for "blind dogs for the guides"!

He then went on to introduce me as "A shining wit" and nobody knew if that was a spoonerism or not!"

Alternatively, I might poke a bit of fun at my host such as:

"Your Chairman has had a pretty torrid day he was telling me. When he got home last night his dog was sitting in the front room with next doors pet rabbit in its mouth. He dragged it out of the dog's mouth and then stuck it in the washing machine to clean it and then blow dried it. Under the cover of night he then snuck over the fence and put it back in the hutch. He then desperately wanted to avoid the neighbour the following morning but alas, as he came out of his front door so did his neighbour. Trying to hide his guilt your Chairman said to his neighbour:

"Are you ok?"

He was then dismayed when the neighbour said:

"No". There are some really sick b.......d's around. Our pet rabbit died yesterday and we buried it in the garden. Some warped individual has only gone and dug him up and put him back in the hutch!"

I use the jokes not as a trial of a stand-up comedy routine, but to relax the audience and to let them know they can laugh. I would then go back to my acronym and start off with:

"The first letter "S" stands for self and sport and go on to talk about my sense of self and how this was challenged when I had my accident. I spent the first few years adjusting to my disability combating the attitudes of the people around me. I had to restore my sense of self-respect, self-belief, and build up my self-confidence.

People, when I was a child would talk about me as though I couldn't hear them. I remember getting on the bus with my mum when I was aged ten soon after my accident, and heard other passengers say:

"Poor little sod". I remember asking my Mum, "Who's got on the bus that we should feel sorry for?"

I then got really angry when it turned out to be me!

I was therefore determined from a very early stage in adjusting to my disability, that I would challenge concepts and prejudices and hopefully use humour to change those views. Sport was the main crutch that I used to plot my progress in my adjustment. I firstly wanted to understand what my abilities were, and using sport, I could set myself limited goals or challenges, which only I would know whether I had succeeded or failed to achieve. It was really important in those early days not to be a failure in anyone's eyes, especially my own. I could set myself a few goals e.g. metres to throw the shot putt or to run in a straight line, and only I would know if I succeeded or not.

I then wanted to challenge the concepts around my disability from my family. I had an aunt who couldn't say any words that might upset me in relation to seeing. She would say "Did you see, watch, hear, the television last night?" I subsequently thought, imagine the situation if I removed the words that might offend someone's sensitivities, it would sound so odd if I said to my friend, "Cheerio Fred, I'll be feeling you". I realise that I might make a few more friends that way but it sounds wrong.

I also talk about how some people focus on your disability rather than your ability. Frequently when I meet people on the tube or walking along the street, they will ask me:

"Do you have a blind dog?"

To which I reply:

"If I had a blind dog, I would have to have another dog to show it where to go!"

The "P" in my acronym would stand for perceptions, and the people that have enabled me to achieve certain things, and of course, the Paralympics.

Here I would talk about the enabling role that people have played in my life. The teacher that supported a particular ambition; the sports coach that enabled me to undertake a mad or potentially dangerous sport; the guy, like Charley, who, in the canoeing, helped me push myself to my physical limits, and all the other guides that allowed me to achieve so much. Perceptions would cover more of the language used by some people and their obsession in either saying the right thing or avoiding saying the wrong thing.

Two examples of this are the guy who met me on the tube one day and, (I hope in his wish to avoid saying anything wrong or use the wrong word regarding my vision), asked me:

"How long have you been unsightly?"!

Or, the Mayoress, who, when introducing me to open a scented garden funded by the local Rotary club, said:

"The blind may not be able to see, but they do smell!"

"O" covers the Olympics and observations. I usually challenge people's observations and say that we often make assumptions, or see something and draw the wrong conclusions. My favourite joke to illustrate this point is the builder interviewing for bricklayers. The builder had an impairment himself in that he had one ear four inches higher than the other, He thought, as a tie break question he would test their powers of observation. He asked each of the candidates how many bricks an hour they could lay, and how long they could do it for? Each of the first 2 gave their answers and when asked the tiebreak question answered that the builder had one ear 4 inches higher or lower than the other. When the third person was asked the tie break question he said: "you wear contact lenses".

When the builder asked him to enlarge upon his answer, he said:

"With ears like that, you can't wear glasses".

"R" covers responses, rights and responsibilities.

"T" incorporates the thoughts or thinking of people, and again, the situations I have been in which either illustrate "their lack of thought" or the inadvertent use of language that has caused me embarrassment.

I was once on the Tube and when we came up above ground, I was frantically flicking backwards and forwards on my portable radio to tune into Radio Five, Sports Extra or Talk Sport. I was so engrossed I forgot which stop I was approaching. I knew that the person next to me was watching and could almost feel their breath on my hands. I turned to him and asked:

"Can you tell me what station this is please"?

He, then grabbed my radio and said:

"Which station are you trying to tune into"?

I was so flabbergasted, I somewhat rudely responded:

"Not the radio station you plonker, which train station are we at?"

Similarly, I was travelling on the tube and had nodded off. I woke up at Aldgate East, where I changed tube lines. The doors were about to close and I said:

"Oh, this is my stop can you hold the doors please?"

I rushed off and as the doors shut a woman on the train said:

"Hold on son, you've left your bag behind"

Someone pulled the door open and passed me my bag, and off went the train. It was then I thought:

"Hold on, I didn't have a bag".

Although it was in the middle of the IRA bombing campaign, I rather stupidly asked a woman on the platform, if she could have a look in the bag to see if there was a bomb in it, as the bag wasn't mine!

She then fled up the platform at a rate of knots and I had no option but to grope in it myself. To my pleasure, I found the bag full of the biggest corn on the cobs I have ever felt! I could just imagine the face of the person on the tube who's bag it was, but it didn't stop me taking the cobs home and eating them.

Another example that backfired on me was when I was trying to cross a busy road in Westminster. I needed help to cross the road and asked a passer-by if he would take me. He said yes, and I asked if I could take his arm? He then astounded me by saying,

"You could, if I had one!"

I thought, what are the odds of a blind man asking a man with no arms to take him over the road! I bought a lottery ticket that night!

The final "S" of SPORTS I finish with, by saying that it stands for state of mind. I recap over the other letters re self, people and perceptions, observations and outlook, reactions and responses, thinking and thought processes, and end by saying that: "Disability is a state of mind, my state and other people's minds; they cannot change my state, but hopefully, I can change their minds".

I also say that, there is nothing funny about disability, but at times, being disabled can be quite funny.

Chapter 10

On the Move Again!

1989

With many regrets I left Islington in 1989 and went to work as a Service Manager in Kensington & Chelsea. The interview again was fraught, with me beating an internal candidate who had been acting up into the job I applied for.

The job interview also involved a series of tests for which my newly developed technology skills were invaluable, and which gave them written evidence of my competence, which was as good as, if not better, than that of the other candidates. Having done well in the interview, they then found it really difficult not to give me the job!

I say that the interview was memorable, in that I turned up to the place where the interview was to be held, and, having been told that we were to do some written tests, asked if I could set my equipment up to save time. I plugged it all in and then found that I would be using a separate room to the other candidates in case the noise of my machines put them off.

My newly mastered special equipment allowed me to complete the exercises and hand in typed written answers and essays. This was a big advantage over the others who handed in barely legible hand written sheets.

The job was to manage an area of the Royal Borough of Kensington and Chelsea, which had been formed by splitting the north of the Borough into two areas covering all services. The other area was to be managed by the manager of the previously combined area. The area covered Notting Hill Gate, and during pre-interview discussions with Alan, the other Service Manager, he told me about some of the issues in the area and what, as a black man doing the job, in a multi-cultural area and with a conservative approach to issues, he thought some of the future challenges might be. My management role would involve supervising managers of residential, day care, home care, children and adult services. I would have up to 9 people reporting to me with several million pounds in my budget.

I met some of the potential reporting managers at the pre interview stage, and I think it must have been difficult for them to give feedback on me as well as remain loyal to the internal candidate who had been managing them. They must have been fair though, as I got through the preliminary stage and then was asked to do the written test and the formal interview.

The written test involved answering some set questions, explaining how you would deal with certain scenarios, and outlining what you would do to win the trust of your staff.

I, for the first time in my working life, had a distinct advantage over my competitors, in that I was using a computer and they were not. I found the test questions straightforward, and managed to write a reasonable amount re the issues and scenarios. I felt going into the interview that, the interview panel had some independent evidence of my written and thinking abilities, which would hopefully counteract any prejudices or misconceptions they might have re my disability and how I would cope.

I enjoyed the interview and even managed to bring a smile to the Panels' faces with my answer to one of their questions. Having worked in Tower Hamlets, Hackney and Islington, I had been expecting an "equal opportunities approach" to the questions. I was therefore somewhat surprised to be asked: "The Royal Borough has a colour blind approach to the provision of its services, what issues do you think this might raise for you?"

I answered without thinking: "With the other co-manager Alan being black, and me being blind, you really would have a colour-blind approach".

I got the job, and was immediately impressed with Kensington's pre-employment approach in relation to wanting to get any specialist equipment in place before I started work. This was the first time that had happened in any of my four previous jobs. I was then told that the internal candidate had not taken the decision well to appoint me, and the personnel officer asked whether it would be o.k. for them to arrange an induction for me which would involve me not being based in the office I was to work in. This would apparently enable the incumbent member of staff to be moved gracefully to a new job and location.

I arrived for work and was given a desk in the Under 5's section of an office in the main town hall. Ironically this was the office that the internal candidate was eventually moved to, and was the service she finally managed. My new staff would travel to my temporary office about 2 miles away from them, and ask me to sign documents or agree payments. Not the start to the new job I had hoped for, but it gave me a chance to see how other sections of the Department worked, and to get to know a wide range of staff outside the area office in which I was to work for the next 11 years.

After 2 weeks or so I was allowed into the building I was to work in. It was a strange one in that it was built into the stilts or supports of the A40 motorway. The Westway flyover, as it is more commonly known, was my building's roof. It is the only place I have ever worked where, when we had a leak in our roof, we had to report it to the Department of Transport. Every minute of the day you heard a "boom boom" noise and felt the building shudder as a vehicle went over the expansion joints or whatever in the road above. When a big lorry came over, the whole building shook, and initially it was very disconcerting. Amazingly however I did get used to it and after a time didn't notice it at all.

I had quite a large office which also doubled as a meeting room. There appeared to be a lot of rubbish left by the previous occupant, with the room seemingly used as a play room presumably for children attending the office with their parents. There were a number of dolls under the desk and bits of broken toys, which after a few days with nobody coming to claim them or use them, I threw into my bin.

The day I dumped everything, a social worker popped her head around my door and asked if it would be o.k. later that day to use my office for a disclosure interview with a child who might have been sexually abused. She also said that she would need the "anatomically correct dolls" which were stored under my desk. I said yes fine and after she had gone rushed to my bin and retrieved all the dolls from the bin and the black rubbish sack I had dumped them in.

I then locked the door to prevent anyone coming in, and proceeded to examine each of the dolls. I pulled their knickers down, or trousers, to see if they had a willy or a vagina and promptly placed the dolls back under the desk. It wasn't until half way through my examination that I suddenly had an awful thought, suppose someone opposite my office could see me through my window from their flat. Imagine the headline:

"Social work manager found guilty of interfering with anatomically correct dolls"

I initially found the role of the Area Manager there a bit lonely and isolated. I had worked in my previous job for nearly six years and had forgotten that it took time to build up trust and relationships. I had been popular and had organised all of the office social functions, which had given me a chance to meet and socialise with people outside my immediate work setting.

In comparison to the new Kensington setup, my old area team had been small. I now had 9 managers to supervise, with 3 of them on different sites. A number of the managers and staff were still very unsure of me in relation to my disability.

Having struggled to master my technology I found myself in the odd position of having to learn how to delegate more and more of my administrative work to my personal assistant. Yes, I had a PA, which was more difficult for me to cope with than you might imagine. They would do anything for me, but I had a number of hang ups in that I was worried about what they might think. Would they think I was giving them a task to do, because I couldn't do it myself, rather than it was something they should be doing? In particular, I found it difficult to ask them to do small personal tasks such as making me or my guests, a cup of coffee or tea.

These issues seem silly now looking back, but were very real at the time. As I grew into the job most of these issues became, either easier to deal with, or disappeared completely.

Working in the Royal Borough, (as I was repeatedly told it had to be referred to), was a fantastic experience, and really challenged me in aspects of my life. I faced many managerial challenges there, such as relocations, a possible outbreak of Legionnaires disease, pigeon flea infestation, the building being over-run with mice, the suicide of a member of staff, disciplinaries and dismissals, reorganisations, oh and of course, the odd social work issue.

Chapter 11

Managing Sport and Social Work: is it a good combination?

1989-93

This period of my life was summed up by the three S's – social work, speaking and sport!

I found that my developing skills and experience in sports management and administration were transferable to my work situations and vice versa. I managed the cross country team at the Winter Paralympics in 1988 in Austria. This was a bit of an additional challenge as the venue we were to use near Innsbruck didn't have any snow! We had to travel by coach or train to Seefeld, which had a small amount of the powdery white stuff. The problem was that it was the only snow for miles around and everyone converged there. In those days the Winter Paralympics was a bit of an afterthought and certainly not the inclusive, significant sporting event it now is. There was only a 2.5 kilometre ski course, and the pleasure skiers were not going to let an event like the Paralympics get in the way of their skiing. During the races, we had tourists skiing with their children, and on one occasion, there was a man walking with his dog, which unfortunately decided to have a dump in the middle of the tracks! I have mentioned the importance of the right colour and kind of wax in cross-country skiing earlier, and the dog pooh did nothing for the racers' glide or grip.

In 1990 we travelled to Jackson, New Hampshire, for the 3rd World Championships. For these games we had a team of ten which I managed. The five Norwegian guides flew into Heathrow only hours before the airport shut down to departing long haul flights because of the very high winds on the runways, and the risk that the loading ramps and stairs would be blown over. This tested my management abilities to the full in ways that I had not envisaged.

I had to negotiate an overnight stay in a hotel for all ten of us and then transport to the hotel and back to the airport the following morning. I managed to get the airport to store our luggage and skis until we flew out the next day, and to provide us with toiletries etc. for all the team to use overnight. I was feeling pretty pleased with myself the following evening when the team and I landed in Boston, but unfortunately, my luggage landed In New York! I managed to get the equivalent of £50 worth of dollars out of the airline in compensation to buy clothing until my luggage caught up with me.

I rushed off to the ski store the next day, as the lost case contained all of my ski suits. The average cost of our skin tight one-piece, lycra ski suits was over 200 dollars each, and after buying some other essentials I only had 40 dollars left to spend. The fashion for the ski suits in those days was to wear the brightest most garish colours you could find. Mo walked me round the shop and every time we passed a certain shelf she hurried past. She eventually said that there was virtually nothing in the store for 40 dollars. I asked why she had used the word virtually, as there must have been something. She then admitted that there was one ski suit that was the brightest, gaudiest and most revolting suit she had ever seen. It coincidentally was priced at 40 dollars and I said well I have got to have something, and took it to the counter to buy it.

As I was paying the shop assistant was saying that it was a bargain as it had been reduced from 160 dollars to 40. He then burst into fits of laughter. He was virtually speechless, and could barely get his breath for laughing. As I gave him my money I asked him what the big joke was. As the tears rolled down his face he eventually pulled himself together and said that it was a standing joke with all the shop assistants in the store that the suit was so awful, only a blind man would ever buy it, and here I was!!!

Those games saw our number one skier, Peter, win our first gold medal in cross country skiing. I think I may have cried even more than I had in Austria, when Peter stood on the podium and they played the national anthem. We all sang "God save the Queen" and even the Norwegians joined in, as the tune was their "King's song", and we had tutored them until they were word perfect with the English words.

In 1992 I managed the team in Albertville, France. I had by then helped to establish the British Paralympic Association (BPA), which was trying to assume responsibility for the Paralympic teams (both summer and winter). Up until 1993, the responsibility had been with the individual disability organisations. I became the Chairman of the national sports body for the visually impaired in the UK - British Blind Sport (BBS), and in 1993, as their Chairman, I signed the agreement ceding responsibility from BBS for all aspect of the multi-disabled Olympics (although we weren't allowed to call it that), to the British Paralympic Association.

I therefore became more involved in sport and disability politics, and the administration of elite sport.

This was during a time of big change in my new work setting. The Community Care Act came into being, which separated adult social care from that of children's welfare.

The social work Department in Kensington decided to go through a service review, and announced the new structure on the very day I had brought together, for the first time, all of the services in my area for our own planning day. The result of the review was that the area I was working in would be divided into three service groups 2 for children and one to cover the adult services.

All of the senior managers had to express a preference for which service they wished to manage across the local authority. I plumped for adults, which surprised me and my boss, as the smart money was on me choosing children. I had enjoyed working with the home care teams, had chaired the residential admissions panel, and quite fancied the challenge of managing the newly established H.I.V. & Aids team. I had put the children's team, in the office I was then managing, as my second choice. Another manager had longer service in the Borough than I did, so she was given her first choice of the adult service group and I got my second choice of children and families. I was fine with this as it meant I didn't have to move offices and I already had enough new challenges with my sporting, work and after dinner speaking commitments.

The latter had been going from strength to strength, with the number of requests to speak, outstripping my ability to undertake them all. The requests were also coming from areas not around London and I frequently found myself rushing out of the office for a train, zooming up to, and back from Birmingham or Bristol, and then travelling back home on the underground in the early hours. I would then be up at 6 am in order to leave by 7am and arrive at work by 9am. It was a really busy time and I loved every moment of it. During this time however, I had become increasingly aware that whilst I was busy at work, loved my sport and got a great deal of satisfaction and of course funds, from the after dinner speaking, I had very few hobbies and rarely did anything for myself that I enjoyed or was local to where I lived.

Chapter 12

Round Table: Winning Friends and Influencing People!

1978-93

As my sporting and work careers developed in the late 1970's and through the 1980's, I became acutely aware that I had virtually no friends locally, had no hobbies and wanted to do something just for fun and perhaps somewhat selfishly, for myself and not for others.

I had spoken at the Romford Round Table and had been invited back on occasions to events or meetings. Round Table was formed by an ex Rotarian in Norwich, who felt that there needed to be another "service organisation" but with a focus for those men under 40 in business.

Many of the banks, large companies and insurance firms, had a system of rotating their aspiring young executives or businessmen around the country on a three year cycle. They would then move on up the ladder, gaining different experiences within their business area. His idea was to provide a forum in every town where the young bankers, insurance brokers etc. could meet and have a ready-made business and friendship network.

The first "aim" of the Round Table's Aims and Objects is: "to develop the acquaintance of young men through the medium of their various occupations". Having got them together it was thought that they could then do things within and for their communities, and so the fundraising became a big part of being a Round Tabler. The other pre-requisite was that you had to have a great deal of fun, usually involving drinking a great deal of alcohol! This seemed to suit my need at that time and I was asked to attend the Round Table meetings of the one I had spoken at in the late 1970's. The members were however nervous about taking a blind person into the Table, and my attendance at their meetings was as much to enable the members to meet me and evaluate me before I went for the formal interview.

After some of the work interviews I have had, and described elsewhere, I didn't think this could be that much of a problem. I was wrong however, when one of the Members raised a formal objection to my application on the grounds that he thought I would not, or could not, play an active part in the Round Table's activities. Thankfully, the objection was over-ruled and I became a full member in 1978. It was great fun and I must admit, I did seek to wind up, at every opportunity, the guy who had objected to my membership. He had allocated me the job as Minutes Secretary, not I think to ease me in gently, but to prove his point that I couldn't do even the smallest task. I didn't let on that I had been a shorthand typist and easily wrote down the notes in Braille to transcribe into print when I got home. When the next meeting came around, I distributed the Braille pages of a Radio Times I had cut up, saying they were the minutes. When the "objector" said that they were no good as they couldn't read them, I answered that he had not told me they had to be in print!

I let him stew for a bit and then produced perfectly typed minutes for the members. He knew when he was beaten and we became fairly friendly after that.

Over the 15 years I was a Tabler, our Round table raised hundreds of thousands of pounds for charity, and had a fabulous time doing it. Looking back on it now it usually involved some form of dressing up. For example, I remember dressing up with my fellow Tablers as lifeboat men. We had our sou'westers and wellies on and were touring the pubs of Romford with collecting buckets. A friend and I went into one very dodgy pub and were collecting, when two fairly drunk men asked, whether we were actually lifeboat men! We thought they were joking so said, yes of course, and carried on collecting. My friend was asked, "what even the blind geezer?" To which my friend replied, "Oh yes, he's our Coxswain"

We carried on collecting round the other end of the pub and heard a row breaking out in our wake. One of the drunken men was saying to the other, "He bloody is a lifeboat man his mate told me" We heard raised voices and then a fight broke out, and we legged it as fast as my mate could steer me!

I also remember being dressed as a nurse in tights and a dress, pushing a hospital bed around the streets of Havering. I won't go into details regarding some of the comments and shouts we got, but suffice to say they were quite crude and had nothing to do with the 2 inflated football bladders that I had stuffed down the front of my dress!

I dressed as Pudsey bear for Children in Need and made sure that Pudsey's patch was over my bad eye, and then confused everyone by managing perfectly well when I put another patch over the other eye!

One of Round Table's biggest fund raising events was the annual firework display. As I had been blinded by a firework, I was not that keen on being anywhere near the fireworks, especially outside. In the end they found me the job of announcer in the hut controlling the Tannoy. I gave announcements re lost children, masterminded the music to which the firework display was set off to, (The War of the Worlds Theme of course), and announced the entertainment which we had arranged. We had various minor celebrities or footballers opening the display and lighting the bonfire. One of the most popular parts of the evening was the performance of the local marching band, which had lots of attractive young women members.

They were called the Romford Drum and Trumpet Core, but inevitably were referred to by the Tablers as "The Romford Bum and Crumpet Core". All the time during the build-up to announcing them, I was repeating the mantra "Drum and Trumpet, Drum and Trumpet" and then as soon as I opened the microphone and announced them, I inevitably called them the Romford Bum and Crumpet Core"!

I used my experiences in Round Table and some of the Tablers I had met, as the butt of some of my after dinner stories. They deserve it, believe me.

I remember one occasion when I was speaking to a large Area Meeting of different Round Tables, before I had actually joined Table. I gave, what I thought was a wonderful talk re spatial awareness and the use of the other senses to orientate yourself. I thought that I would get some really good questions, as Round Table was reputedly for the rising young businessmen and executives of the future. They were the potential cutting edge high flyers. Imagine then, my disappointment when, having finished my talk, I asked if anyone had any questions and the room was totally silent. I felt a bit anxious and repeated, "surely someone must have a question?"

When nobody spoke, I gave up and went to sit down. As I did so I heard someone towards the back of the hall click their fingers. I said:

"Great a question at last, yes sir what do you want to ask?"

There was some laughter before he actually got to speak. Apparently, when I had first asked for questions, this thrusting young executive put his hand up! When I again asked if anyone had a question, he began to wave at me! Finally, realising that I couldn't see him, he clicked his fingers to attract my attention. It got worse, however, when he did ask his question ie: "Using your other senses, can you estimate, and tell me, how far from you I am standing?" When I replied, "Sir, I think you are about 60 feet from me", he turned to his colleagues next to him and asked: "Is he right?" He turned out to be a chartered surveyor!

Another memorable occasion was the Round Table Blind Cricket challenge. When I eventually joined Table, I was asked what sports I did and said that my sports club Metro were actually National champions at blind cricket and I was a regular team member. I explained that we used a small football with ball bearings inside to make a noise, rather than a cricket ball, and that the rules were adapted slightly. The totally blind players when they were fielding could catch the ball on the full, or when it had bounced once. When bowling to a blind batsman, the bowler had to say "play" as they released the ball, and the ball had to pitch twice before the crease for the totally blind and once for the partially sighted players. Oh, and the other concession was that the totally blind batsmen could have a runner to run for them (to avoid bloody great pile-ups in the middle of the pitch!).

The Round Table then asked if they could play my blind team and I arranged a match. They still had the slightly condescending attitude towards disability mentioned earlier. As we were getting ready to play I heard from a friend in the opposing dressing room that the captain had indeed given them a very patronising team talk. It went something like:

"Ok lads we are playing Mike's blind team today so let's make a game of it. If they manage to hit the ball at all we can give them four runs for it, and if they manage to get it past a fielder don't run too fast and we can then give them six runs for it, etc. etc."

One lasting memory of Table is, that the thrusting young executives often had a very inflated view of their actual abilities. One Tabler came to the crease to bat complete with pads and a cricket box! What harm an inflated small football could have done to him I can't imagine. He thought he was Donald Bradman reincarnated and took guard. It was very obvious from the outset that the last time he had hit two balls in succession was when he trod on a garden rake! He was out first ball and the Round Table side were 16 runs all out including six extras! I somewhat uncharitably said afterwards that, "The following year we offered to play them in daylight and it made absolutely no difference"!

One of the key features of Round Table was to enable "the young men" to try and experience and achieve things they would not normally have attempted. Romford is twinned with a town in Germany called Ludwigshafen. I think my enjoyment of new challenges must have rubbed off on my fellow Tablers as we decided to do a sponsored bike ride from Romford to Ludwigshafen. It was 500 miles and we planned to do it in five days with some of the Tablers doing parts of the route in a relay and me doing it all on a tandem. We then sold tickets whereby people guessed what the mileage was and the one nearest to the distance won £50. I had ridden on a tandem a few times but never the distances each day involved in the challenge. The key issue was to find me a front rider who could do the distance, be confident and happy about having a blind rider on the back, and someone who I could get on with. Weeks went by and still no guide had been found. One was identified but was on holiday and was due back a few days before we were due to set off. I phoned regularly over those days but couldn't get hold of him, and in the end, we had to agree to meet up on the day we started the ride and hope that there weren't any problems. I wasn't sure what clothing to wear for such a long journey and settled on my most comfortable track suit and running shorts underneath.

When we met in the car park of Romford Town Hall, I got on the back seat of the tandem which my front rider Roy had adjusted, and we toured the car park. Our balance was pretty good and everything looked great for a good trip.

Roy who, until that point I had never met before, asked me if I was going to get changed. I asked him what he meant and he said aren't you going to wear proper cycling shorts with the built in chamois to avoid chafing etc.? I hadn't a clue what he was talking about and it obviously showed. He explained that when you were undertaking long distance cycling it was easy to develop sores on your bottom and on your groin areas because of the chafing of your clothing. He said that he had a spare pair of cycling shorts and asked if I wanted to use them. I said yes and he handed them over to me. He then said that obviously I wouldn't have any chamois grease to put on and so did I want him to do that for me as well? I again must have looked blank and he explained that to reduce the chance of chafing even more, you smeared fat or grease over the chamois leather to provide some lubrication around the parts a well-known lager cannot reach. I said fine and began to strip off and asked one last stupid question.

"Erm re these shorts, do I have to take my underpants off in order to get the benefit from the fat?"

He of course said yes so I carried on stripping.

Just as I was naked from the waist down, I had an alarming thought: here I was with a man I had never met before in a car park at the back of the town hall with me naked from the waist down and him standing behind me with a pot of grease in his hands"!

This is a demonstration of trust to the highest degree!

One of the funniest and most confusing Table activities for us was the annual Christmas Float. This involved one of us dressing up as Father Christmas, sitting on a trailer bedecked as Santa's Grotto, and shouting "Ho Ho Ho" as you went by. Whilst you did so, your fellow Tablers collected money from the houses and gave the parents sweets for the kids. The trailer was towed by a land rover driven by another Round Tabler.

We managed to confuse the children greatly as, on consecutive nights, they witnessed a Chinese, an Asian and a blind Father Christmas! As I mentioned earlier, most Round Tablers like a drink, and on the Xmas float nights, we met up before we went out and had a few beers to keep out the cold. I kept with tradition and had a couple of drinks or perhaps it was a few more. Needless to say, in the middle of a busy road junction the Land Rover and its trailer, with me on it dressed as Father Christmas, stopped very suddenly. I was off balance, because of the bad driving of course, and not the alcohol, and promptly fell off in the middle of the junction. The driver was oblivious to my plight, or wanted to frighten me, so drove off leaving me in the middle of the traffic. When they came back for me the junction was gridlocked and there were a lot of very concerned motorists wondering how they were going to explain to their children that Santa had gone blind, and even more worryingly, how he would find the chimney let alone get down it with the presents!

I went to Round Table national sporting weekends and represented the Area at swimming and bowls, and also went to the national conference and took part in the debates and also the mass fancy dress parties. The parties were themed and I remember ten of us from Table and our wives, all dressed as owls and pussycats, walking into an off licence and frightening the owner half to death as he thought he was being robbed.

Table provided me with exactly what I needed at that stage in my life. I had great fun, made friends locally to where I lived, and of course raised money for local good causes.

Chapter 13

My Sport or My work: Which is Most Important?

1992-98

I think the answer to the above question was undoubtedly that both were of equal importance to me. This period of my life was both challenging but immensely satisfying. I had become a respected senior manager and one of the most highly paid persons with a disability in local government. My successes in managing the ski team led to me being invited to manage the England blind cricket team in the first world cup of blind cricket in India, and being asked to be the Chef de Mission for the 1998 Winter Paralympic Games in Nagano, Japan.

I had also organised and funded a trip to South Africa to establish blind sport, and in particular cricket, following the fall of apartheid.

I had managed the ski team in the 1992 Paralympic Winter Games in Albertville and the 1994 Games in Norway and had a major reunion of the guides from Norway who had helped us to become a significant competing cross country team. I was also the only Board member of the British Paralympic Association representing winter sports and winter sport athletes, and was helping to establish elite sport for people with disabilities as being exactly that, namely sport first and disability second.

This was probably one of the most hectic times to date. My involvement with the BPA was increasing significantly. As well as managing various sports teams, and competing, I was increasing my involvement in getting the sports that I was connected to, included in their mainstream, non-disabled, sporting governing bodies. I had announced that my racing career would end in Lillehammer, Norway, 20 years almost to the week that it had started in Beitostolen, Norway.

On the last night, following yet another successful event with our no. 1 skier winning another bronze medal, we held a get together with the team and virtually all of the Norwegian guides who had helped us over that 20 year period. It was full of speeches, a bit emotional and it felt like a bit of an ending.

They say, as one door closes another opens. As mentioned above, I was asked to manage other sports teams such as the blind athletics team which competed in European and world championships, and then the England blind cricket team which was to compete in the first world cup in India. Anyone who has ever travelled to India knows just how much a challenge it is to personally cope with your own emotions and feelings, let alone trying to understand the culture, eat and drink things that you have never experienced, and ensure you keep well. If you add to this, watching over and managing 20 other blokes, none of whom had ever visited India before, then you may get an idea of what I took on!

Nothing I think had prepared the team for the squalor, poverty, teeming humanity, and the overwhelming generosity of the people they met. In many ways, because of this, it is an ideal place for the blind to visit. I was once asked what my lasting memories of India were. I replied: "Whilst there, I heard a lot, smelt a lot and trod in a lot."

Then came the pinnacle of my sports management career to that point. I was asked to be the Chef de Mission (in other words the head honcho) for the 1998 Winter Paralympic Team in Nagano, Japan.

Unfortunately this again was not the joyful experience it might have been, in that a few months before we were due to fly out, I snapped my anterior cruciate ligament! (Yes the same one that I did ten years earlier). I had two operations including a ligament replacement, and by the time we boarded the plane I had a leg brace firmly clamped to my leg, crutches (with retractable spike tips on the bottom for the snow) and plenty of pain killers.

The ligament had been snapped whilst playing football. I went to trap the ball and instead of putting my foot behind the ball I put it on top; as I fell my knee turned inwards, and my stomach went over as I heard a pistol like crack as the ligament completely snapped this time.

As the manager of a multi-disabled ski team, many of whom are paralysed or have limbs missing, it would have been a bit difficult to pull out of the trip because I had a bad leg! The team was a fairly large one and included over 50 athletes, staff, guides and medical staff. There were 3 winter sports disciplines to cover – cross-country skiing, alpine skiing and sledge hockey.

Despite what you might think from the various trips abroad mentioned above, I was incredibly committed to, and enjoying my work. I did however try my employer's patience by having to have 3 months off work with the snapped ligament, and then got them to preserve my sanity by rescuing me from the boredom at home and paying for me to travel to work each day via minicab. I had prided myself that, in the 8 years I had been with Kensington I had not had a single days sickness and then I took 3 months in one go!

I had, during this period to manage significant cuts to budgets. There was also a move to recognise those in need of social work help or the recipients of social work intervention, as consumers and not clients. I introduced complaints procedures and initiated feedback mechanisms regarding our services.

I was busy managing sports teams, various social work teams and was undertaking more and more after dinner speaking and presentations at conferences, but became increasingly aware that I had few, if any hobbies and had nothing to replace my activities with Round Table which I had left, because of the age rule, in 1993. I did nothing purely for enjoyment or fun and which was local to where I lived.

Chapter 14

The Pinnacle: Top Job at Work and Play
1998-2001

In 2000 I was made Assistant Director within Kensington following a further reorganisation, and in the same year went to the Sydney Paralympic Summer Games as a director of BPA, and was approached to see whether I would consider standing for the Chairmanship of BPA when the elections took place in late 2000 or early 2001. This position I got elected to, and became the first Chairman with a disability and the first ex athlete to hold the position.

The Chairmanship was a voluntary position but involved many hours of meetings and a fair amount of foreign travel. I was undertaking more and more after dinner speaking. Whilst this was not a local interest, the speaking became the hobby replacing Round Table. It was not relaxing but I had a great deal of fun doing it, raised considerable funds for my charities, and met some very interesting people. The day job was challenging and took increasing amounts of time i.e. leaving at 7 am and getting home after 8 most evenings. I was travelling between 3 and 4 hours a day on the Underground, and feeling somewhat overwhelmed with the work, sporting and speaking commitments; something had to give and I decided that perhaps it was time to think about a new job, out of social work, and possibly in the voluntary sector.

I am really not sure whether the above is a rationalisation of how I was feeling at that time or whether I just felt that I needed yet another new challenge. I realised on the one hand that I was envied by many friends and colleagues with a disability who said that I was mad to even think of giving up voluntarily the wonderful job I had striven for so many years to obtain. On the other hand however, having succeeded in getting the jobs I had applied for, I then had the confidence to believe that I could do something else. I had been a senior manager for over 11 years and was becoming disillusioned and less stimulated by the things I was having to do on a day to day basis at work. I think I missed the client contact and felt that I was on a treadmill. Someone else had their finger on the speed control that governed how fast I ran. I thought that I could run faster but didn't want to. I also realised that the faster you run the more chance there was of coming off, so I wanted to choose both the speed of my day to day life and whether I stepped, rather than was pushed, off the work treadmill.

I also hit 50 in 2000, so was probably in the frame of mind that started to take stock and make choices about what I wanted to do, rather than what

I had to do. The highlight of this period however, had to be my attending the Sydney Paralympic Games in Australia. I had attended 7 Winter Paralympic Games but not a summer games. As, in 2000 I was a long serving director of the British Paralympic Association, and someone with experience of Paralympic Games, I was asked to go as part of the management support team. The Chef de Mission was new to the job and Australia was definitely the furthest we had ever travelled with the team and it was uncertain what demands would be made on the Chef and the wider management team.

The Games were on a significantly larger scale than the winter games. There were 4000 athletes from over 130 countries, plus several thousand coaches and support staff. Our team was the largest we had produced, and the pressure was on us to improve on our 4th position at the previous Games. It was during the Games that I learned that the Chairman of BPA was not going to stand at the forthcoming elections. I was sounded out by a number of people whether I would consider allowing my name to go forward as a possible candidate. Seeing the success in Sydney, and the opportunities that sport had given so many people with disabilities to achieve their dreams and showcase their abilities, I had no hesitation in agreeing, as I wanted to ensure that more people had those opportunities.

The highs were also counter-balanced by some heart-breaking issues that I found myself dealing with at work. One in particular made me re-evaluate what my priorities were re never knowing what is around the corner. One of my social workers was the ex-wife of a very famous musician. Her son was following in his dad's musical career and was in a band with the son of another famous artist. With no warning, the social worker's son died, I think from an asthma attack. He was in his early 20's and she was completely devastated. She went off sick and after several months was still an emotional mess and couldn't come back to work. I eventually had to convene a panel and dismiss her as we needed to fill the vacancy to provide the service. At about the same time, one of the cases that I had been overseeing broke down, and my Department had to remove the four children of a woman with moderate learning disabilities. It proved impossible to place the children together, and the mother assaulted the social worker in court and so we then had to decide whether to take action against the mother!

Having to deal with these type of issues were not uncommon and I think the constant drip of human misery and evidence of abuse and family breakdown was probably wearing me down. I had been working in social work for 27 years and I started to feel that my "sell by date" had arrived.

Funny things though still happened to me to provide material for my after dinner speaking and to keep me smiling. On the way to work, for example, I rushed down onto the platform of the Tube to find that the train was in and just about to close its doors. I got to the train and stuck my white stick out between the doors to prevent them closing or to stop them closing fully. Imagine my surprise therefore, when the driver didn't open the doors and the train then started to leave the platform with my white stick firmly grasped in the doors. White sticks are made up of four or five sections joined together by some thick elastic. As the train pulled out the elastic started to stretch, and stretch and stretch. I couldn't hold on any longer and let go of the stick and heard it clattering on the side of the train as it zoomed off. The people around me were worried about how I would cope without a stick, I was however in fits of laughter as I was imagining the faces of the people at the next station when the stick drops out of the door with no blind person attached! Would they look under the train? I soon stopped laughing and had to work out what I needed to do to continue my journey. I got one of the passengers to take me to the staff by the ticket barrier and asked them if by any chance they had access to their cleaning cupboard. They did and I was extremely grateful to the station supervisor who agreed to my suggestion that he broke the broom handle off the cleaner's broom and allowed me to use it as a stick. It was brown and not white but you can't have everything in life.

My journey to and from work was another factor in my thinking that I needed a change of jobs to one nearer home. I started to apply during this period for Director of Children's Services posts near to where I lived. I then saw a job advert for something in the voluntary sector. It was to set up a new charity with a focus on bringing together professionals from health, social care and the not for profit sector, with a focus on prevention of sight loss and blindness or, supporting those where prevention wasn't possible but for whom ameliorating the effects of sight loss was the key issue. I had prided myself that all my working life had been in non-disability related occupations and wasn't sure how I felt about working with sight loss when I was vision impaired myself.

I decided in the end, not to apply for the charity post and to keep my fingers crossed that something would turn up.

So in 2001, I was Chairman of the British Paralympic Association and I had a well-paid, demanding and responsible job as Assistant Director for children's services in Kensington; my dilemma was could I do both adequately?

Chapter 15

Chairing, Chief Execing and Championing
2001-2003

This two year period was again very busy and exciting. I had been applying, and being shortlisted, for Director of Children's Services positions, and was runner up on 3 occasions. Had I hit the glass ceiling re my ambition in social work?

I think it was Mr. Micawber who said "Something will turn up", well in my case it did. The job in the voluntary sector, which I had decided not to apply for, came up again and I was approached to apply. I decided that I was indeed ready for a change and sent in my application. The interview (unlike virtually every other job interview I had experienced to that date) went well, and I went home with my fingers crossed feeling that *I had done ok*. Talk about waiting for buses and then two come along together! On the day I heard that I had got the job in the voluntary sector, I was told that I had made it to the last 3 candidates for the Director of Children's Services post in a large county authority. I asked the charity if I could go to the social work interview and then let them know once I had heard re the Director post. They luckily understood my dilemma and agreed to hold the job open until I knew the result.

Throughout my time in Kensington, I was wonderfully supported by a lady that would read everything to me including my post, children in care reviews, hi-fi magazines and sports results. Betty had originally lived in Islington and then moved to Kent, but still travelled in regularly to read to me. I asked her if she would accompany me to the test part of the preliminary interviews as the county's HR department said they could not guarantee that all the tests were in an accessible format. There were psychometric tests, tests involving pie charts, and one involving a mass of diagrams and spread sheets, where I would have to compare data and identify trends. Betty was immensely worried that she would let me down by not describing something properly or give me the wrong information.

I would challenge anyone, for example, to try looking at a pie chart and describe what proportion of it is shaded compared with another pie chart. They had managed to Braille out some of the information which consisted of 15 tables, each on a separate sheet, which I then had to draw comparisons from or Inter-link blocks of data. I had to spread the sheets across the whole of a table top and stand up to reach all of them. I then, after 2 hours of tests, met some of the staff, by which time I was mentally drained and probably didn't sparkle.

I was fairly pessimistic on the way home. I didn't think I had done that brilliantly with the test and had only completed about half of it, as I had run out of time. This was definitely due to the time taken of having the information spoken to me, rather than the difficulty of the problems to be solved. I didn't think that I would be called back for the final interview. I was wrong however, and was shortlisted to attend interview the day after the Charity job interview.

I explained to the Charity Chairman, that I had spent 27 years in social work and thought that I needed to at least give it one last shot i.e., obtaining the top job. The Chair was very understanding and said that I could let them know once I knew the outcome of the final interview. Needless to say, I was runner-up again to an internal candidate and decided to accept the Development Director post with mixed emotions.

The job of setting up a new charity was a great challenge but, was I ready to work in the disability sector with vision impairment?

When I met with my Director of Children's Services in Kensington to hand in my notice, I was really touched at the genuine emotion shown re my decision. I was even more overwhelmed when Kensington offered me the option of a safety net, in that they proposed a 2 year secondment, whereby I kept all my employment terms and conditions with the Royal Borough, the charity paid my reduced salary to Kensington, and that, if things didn't work out, I would have a job in Kensington to return to.

I started the new job as Development Director of VISION 2020 UK at the end of September 2001, some six months after being elected as Chairman of the British Paralympic Association.

Having got over the elation of being elected Chairman, I soon realised what it was that I had taken on. Despite our success in Sydney, the BPA was virtually bankrupt. The Chief Executive and virtually all of the temporary staff recruited for the Games, had left, and the remaining 5 members of staff felt anxious and leaderless. With the help of an administrator, herself a temp, who, thankfully had agreed for her contract to be renewed several times, I set up, and undertook interviews for the new staff, including the new CEO. I then drafted contracts, undertook inductions, and attended staff meetings to reassure the remaining staff. This, at times, felt like a full-time job instead of the voluntary commitment I had entered into. It didn't help matters that the office was in Croydon and I was in Essex, so the travel took up a lot of time. There was also an additional sense of urgency in that the Winter Paralympics in Salt Lake City were only a few months away and we needed someone urgently to oversee the preparation of, and the arrangements for, the team to train, travel and compete.

The 2002 Winter Paralympics took place some six months into my new job. I took a few days leave to attend as Head of Delegation, but it was with very mixed emotions. There were no cross country skiers in the team as our top skier, Peter, had sadly been diagnosed with cancer, and his prognosis was poor. These were the first winter Games that I had not been integrally involved in organising part or all of the British team's participation, and I had to admit to myself that I missed the action.

After the Games, the new job of setting up VISION 2020 UK soon focussed my mind. I managed to get a number of the bigger charitable organisations to put in some start-up funding of £20,000 each. I then got a membership structure and subscription rates agreed, and drafted a constitution for submission to the Charities Commission. The membership criteria established was that any international, national or regional body, with a primary focus on issues to do with sight, or sight loss, could apply to join. Each organisation would then pay a subscription based on their annual income, and that all would have the same voting rights. We wanted to encourage cross sector working, and encouraged applications from professional bodies in the health and allied services, from social care, from the not for profit sector and from organisations of the vision impaired. We wanted to become a neutral body under whose umbrella different organisations could work together and collaborate. Much of the early work plan of the charity had been formulated by two other bodies working with similar aims and objectives, and had disbanded when the new organisation was formed. The charity didn't even have a name to put on the application form to the Charities Commission.

In 2001, the World Health Organisation (WHO), commenced a global initiative called "VISION 2020". The aims were to eradicate avoidable blindness around the world by the year 2020, and A further objective was to establish country and regional "VISION 2020's". These bodies would include any organisation focussing on issues to do with sight loss prevention, or the amelioration of the effects of living with sight loss. These objectives seemed to be exactly what we were proposing to do, and so we applied to be VISION 2020 UK under the WHO global plan. Our application was accepted and the UK became the second national committee formed.

I then began to look for collaborative projects that perhaps VISION 2020 UK could help with. There had been, for example, a number of charities discussing putting in a bid for funds to undertake a major piece of research into the lives and aspirations of vision impaired people. The seven charities who met, could not agree which one of them should lead the bid on behalf of the others, and felt that the preference would be, for a neutral body to bid on behalf of all the organisations and thus no single charity would take the limelight and the risk. The new charity that I was leading had been set up exactly for that kind of role, and surprisingly, they all agreed for me to lodge the research bid to the Big Lottery Fund. The fact that my charity was not actually, as such, registered as a charity at the time of submitting the bid, was thought to be a big problem and I redoubled my efforts to get the registration agreed. I think nobody was more surprised than me, when we were awarded a grant of just under half a million pounds, the day after the charity was formally registered.

I managed, when I started the new job, to get some further assistance from the Access to Work Programme for equipment and to cover the costs of a reader/facilitator. Betty still struggled over from Kent but it gradually became apparent that I would need more administrative support than just reading, and as the charity expanded I thought it might be able to employ someone. Betty, was then in her early seventies, and she and I agreed to end our work partnership, but have remained friends to this date.

One interesting aspect of my new Development Director role, was working with, and reporting to, a Board of Trustees. This experience occurred some six months after having become a Chairman of a Board of Trustees to whom a Chief Executive reported! It felt a bit schizophrenic but immensely useful, in that I could use the experience both ways, i.e. know what information I needed, and how I wanted it presented as a Chairman, and then kept this in mind when I was presenting material to my Chairman and the Board.

I was enjoying my roles as a Chief Executive of one charity, and Chairman of another, and certainly had enough challenges and excitement in my life. I then received a phone call in my capacity as Chairman of BPA, asking me if I would meet a representative of the British Olympic Association (BOA) and someone linked to the Sports Council. I thought it might be to do with some additional funding, or to try and establish closer links to the BOA, so of course said yes.

When we met I was thrilled to find out that the subject of our discussions was whether BPA would support BOA in a late bid to host the 2012 Olympic and Paralympic Games! I think I did know that the bidding arrangements had changed in that up until the process to select the host city for the summer Games in 2012, the bidding cities could decide not to host the Paralympics as well. The fact that since 1988, all the cities, had hosted the Paralympics, was to their immense credit, but was not compulsory. Without even asking what "supporting a bid" would involve, I said that I felt sure my Board would agree and then hurriedly contacted them to ensure that I was right.

The bid was duly submitted and I was asked if I would serve on the company that would be the Bid Board. I went and met Barbara Cassani who was to chair the bid board, in the newly acquired office on the 50th floor of 1 Canada Square. I then attended my first Board meeting in October 2003 and as the members of the Board introduced themselves I must admit I was completely overawed. Here were business men such as Sir Howard Bernstein who had masterminded the successful 2002 commonwealth Games; sportsmen such as Sir Steve Redgrave, Dalton Grant and Seb Coe; the CEO and Chairman of the BOA; oh and of course, Princess Anne!

I felt that I was moving in higher circles, not just because we were meeting on the 50th floor of 1 Canada Square, but because, in order not to miss the first Board meeting I had flown back from holiday in Spain for the day and was due to fly back after the meeting. I am not sure if I spoke at the initial Board, which for those of you that know me, is most unusual. Thus started my involvement over the next 9 years with the bid for, preparation and delivery of, the London 2012 Olympic and Paralympic Games.

During this period I also lost 2 close friends. They were both blind from birth with the childhood cancer Retinal Blastoma. They had been at school with me and then were founder members, with me, of my sports Club Metro. They then both became international athletes in their own right and attended the trials with me to compete for Britain in the first Winter Paralympics. All three of us were selected, and competed in the Games, and became the catalyst of the Paralympic Winter sports cross-country ski team which was to have so much success later. They were both in their mid-40's when they died from a recurrence of cancer, which I subsequently learned was a not uncommon feature of their original condition. This really did shock me. How two extremely fit and able sportsmen could suddenly be cut down and disabled further by an awful disease, it just didn't seem fair.

It had the effect of reaffirming my decision to enjoy life to the full, and to seek new challenges where I could, and to do new things for as long as I was able.

Chapter 16

I had to Pinch Myself

2003-05

I was now a Director serving on the London 2012 Bid Board, and planning how we would stage the Games if we won the bid, and the strategy of influencing key IOC members and ultimately presenting to the Games Commission as to why London should hold the games.

This was a really exciting period of my life. I suppose I was a bit star struck working with so many legends of sport on the bid. The formal submission took the form of a book that covered every section of the template laid down by the IOC. We had to cover health and medical provision, accommodation for athletes and officials, hotel availability and pricing for visitors and spectators, and the transition from Olympic to Paralympic Games. The book was over 2 feet thick and that was just what we had to do to be accepted as a Candidate City. There were, I think, 9 cities in the original first round, and they then whittled that down to a final short list of 5 cities – London, Madrid, Paris, New York and Moscow. We had to obtain the full backing of the British Government and the leaders of the opposition parties, the Mayor's office and the London Assembly.

Whilst I was somewhat in awe of my fellow Board members, I became increasingly uneasy and eventually extremely vocal about their inability to think and talk about the Paralympics as well as the Olympics. Their inability was mirrored, at that time, by the Minister responsible for the Games, who also in every speech that she made just mentioned "the Olympics" and never referred to the Paralympics.

Some of the bid team flew out to the 2004 Athens Paralympics and things improved a bit after that but not much. The 2012 Games in London were being billed by the bid team, as the first truly inclusive Games. The Games would provide easy access for spectators to the stadiums, for both Olympics and Paralympics, for people with disabilities. Our planning would be fully integrated to make the transition from one Games to the other seamless and easy. So why the heck couldn't the key people driving the process get it into their heads to think and talk inclusively about "the Olympic and Paralympic Games"?

Some said that when they said "Olympic" they used the word generically, to cover both, but I didn't believe them. There was a lot of mistrust from the disability sports bodies who had largely been either excluded or ignored by their non-disabled sporting counterparts. I had to try and convince the Paralympic sports leaders and athletes that the Games would be truly inclusive, whilst at the same time, I was being contradicted by the key leaders of the bid by their failure to mention Paralympics on any occasion they spoke about the Games!

Mo was aware of my frustration and was relieved when I came home from a Board meeting following the trip to Athens and said that for the first time I thought the Board had "got it". The reports from the staff who had attended their first Paralympic games in 2004 were positive and full of their experiences, and raved how fantastic the Games were. They were fired up to ensure that if we won the bid, our Games would truly be "the best ever".

Mo and I then went the following day to a reception where the speakers were, Seb Coe, the London Mayor, and the "Olympics" Minister. BPA were asked to ensure that a number of our Paralympic athletes were present and a number of our wheelchair athletes and blind runners were present and visible. During all three speeches, not a single mention or reference was made to the Paralympics. After the speeches finished Seb came over to Mo and I and asked what I thought of what they had said. I think he could see I was not very happy and I think I said "not a lot". Seb then looked at Mo and said: "Oh gosh I didn't mention Paralympics".

Mo, who is normally shy and retiring, perhaps fortified by a glass of wine, tore into him. With all the Paralympic athletes evident in front of him, she asked if he was blind as well as deaf? He then replied that he was sorry and that he was tired. Mo then said what a feeble excuse and that we were all tired, having all been in Greece for the previous 3 weeks.

This totally unexpected outburst did more to ram the issue home than all my diplomatic efforts. I am not sure Seb was used to being spoken to like that, but it certainly had the necessary effect. When I next attended a major event where Seb was speaking he talked about "Olympic and Paralympic Games" and then added that he had specifically mentioned "Paralympic" otherwise, if he had not, Mike Brace's wife would kill him!

I don't want to labour the point too much but I think this was the breakthrough that laid the foundation for the approach to the London 2012 Games and that did, indeed, make them the most inclusive games to date.

The 2004 Athens Paralympics were my first summer Games as Head of Delegation. I went to the holding camps in Cyprus and then attended the Games throughout. The venues were finished very late and we were particularly worried how they would be converted from Olympic to Paralympic operation mode. The Greeks had made great efforts to make Athens more accessible, with even the Acropolis having a degree of wheelchair accessibility.

A big concern was the drivers and the transport. Pavements were very high and uneven. Wheelchair access points on and off the pavements were considered to be a major issue, and nobody had a solution to the attitude and behaviour of the average Greek driver, i.e. park anywhere and keep death off the roads, by driving on the pavements!

The city authorities made a brave effort to accommodate the hundreds of wheelchair users expected in Athens by installing a number of sloped areas or dropped pavements. Unfortunately, the drivers saw these installations as easier pathways for them to drive up onto the pavements or park off road!

The BPA had become much more professional in its approach to the Games and the preparation of its athletes and staff. The BPA gets no state funding and we had managed to raise the hundreds of thousands of pounds needed to pay for the training and holding camps, the flights to and from Cyprus and Athens, accommodation costs outside the village, and equipment. The team finished second in the medal table, winning more medals than in Sydney and in more sports. This was the highest placing for Great Britain at any Paralympic Games to date!

Despite my involvement with the Olympic and Paralympic bid, and my significant and growing involvement with the British Paralympic Association, I was really enjoying my work as Chief Executive of VISION 2020 UK. My secondment had expired at the end of September 2003, and I decided that I would stick with the voluntary sector rather than face going back into social work. I did struggle however with the fact that I was blind and was now working in the area of blindness and sight loss, which I had always vowed I would never do. When considering a career change I had even considered becoming a professional after dinner speaker, i.e. doing it as a job and taking the money for myself instead of giving it to my charities. I had decided not to pursue this pathway as I rationalised that the main reason I was booked to speak, I thought, was because I was disabled. I did not want to become, or be thought of, as a professional disabled person, but considered myself a professional, who had a disability.

By 2004, however, I had worked through this and did feel that I could make a difference in vision impaired people's lives by enabling them and empowering them, to have some or all of the life chances that had been open to me. Someone once said "information is power" and working for VISION 2020 UK brought home to me just how information starved most vision impaired people are. People with a vision impairment could not see advertisements for products or information posters on the underground or other public display areas. Many, if not most websites were not accessible to people with a vision impairment. Most of the thousands of magazines, books and journals produced each year were not available in accessible formats. Until comparatively recently, vision impaired people could not get a daily or weekly newspaper in a format they could read. When audio books were produced, they were five times the cost of the printed version. Hospital or doctors' appointment letters are still not usually sent in an accessible format.

I also at this time became aware of the demographics and prevalence of sight loss in the UK. The majority of those experiencing sight loss do so after the age of 50. Two of the main causes of sight loss, Cataracts and Macular Degeneration, account for a significant proportion of those with sight loss and these conditions are particularly found in older people. Another major cause of sight loss is Diabetes, leading to in some cases, Diabetic Retinopathy. With diabetes on the increase nationally, the numbers with Diabetic Retinopathy are set to snowball. There is also significant co-morbidity with other disabilities such as hearing loss, especially in the elderly.

Part of my role as CEO of VISION 2020 UK was to improve the information access to vision impaired people, and to raise awareness of sight loss and its impact on the lives of thousands of people. Sight Loss is often referred to as a hidden disability and as probably 95 per cent of those with a vision impairment can see something, it is not surprising that their issues and problems are overlooked or not considered.

The other shocking thing I learned in those early days was that something like 80 per cent of the world's blindness could be eradicated. The cures or treatment drugs are already available, but the delivery mechanisms are not set up in the countries that have the eye conditions. The biggest threat to sight for millions of children, for example, is the lack of vitamin "A".

Almost as a bit of light relief, from the job and Paralympics, was an expansion in my after dinner speaking activities. Much of the money I raised now went to the British Paralympic Association, and I had been asked to become a trustee of the Primary Club (The cricketers' charity that raises money to provide sports and recreational facilities for the visually impaired) and I therefore ensured that they also got their fair share of my fundraising efforts.

I then, in early November 2005, received one of the strangest phone calls I had ever experienced. In early November I picked up the telephone and a cultured voice on the other end asked if I was Mr. Brace. Having replied yes, the caller then said that she was ringing from No. 10 Downing Street. I almost laughed and put the phone down but listened when she said that I had been sent a letter, but they believed it had gone astray. The content of the letter was to say that the Prime Minister was minded to recommend to the Queen that I be awarded the Order of the British Empire (OBE) in the 2005 New Year's Honours List. I was gob smacked! She then went on to say that because of the delay I only had until 24th November to respond to say whether I accepted the nomination. I was, of course, extremely honoured, but felt a bit of a fraud in that I had loved every minute of my work in sport, and therefore it felt a bit odd to get rewarded for it. I was told that I couldn't tell anyone, and the next I would hear would be when it was announced in the media.

I managed to keep it secret, apart from telling Mo that is, and had planned to celebrate on New Year's Eve with 2 close friends at my house. Unfortunately my friend Alan's dad died just before Christmas and was not wanting to celebrate the new year. I instead went to my step brother's house as he was having a party. Just as the chimes of Big Ben were about to be heard, I mentioned that I had got the OBE, but it was too late to ring my mum and tell her.

Chapter 17

A Great Honour

2005

Having eventually calmed down re the news of my OBE, I then had to buckle down to prepare my part of the presentation to the International Olympic Committee (IOC) Commission in order for the UK bid to make it through to the final selection round in Singapore. I was told that the date for my trip to the palace to collect the OBE could take months to come through, and as the first key presentation to the IOC was to be in February, there should not be a clash of dates, and there was plenty of time to prepare myself for both events!

I should have known better, as two weeks into the New Year I was told that my trip to the Palace would be on 17th February, the day after the first presentation to the IOC Commission and the day before I, as part of the group with the Commission was also to meet Tony Blair and the leaders of the opposition in the Cabinet Office at No. 10 during the day, and then the Queen, who was hosting a dinner at Buckingham Palace in the evening!!

I therefore found myself on consecutive days:

Presenting to the IOC; travelling to the palace to collect my OBE from the Queen; meeting Tony Blair and the leaders of the opposition in the Cabinet room at No. 10 Downing Street; and attending a dinner in the state banqueting rooms at Buckingham Palace!

I had to summon all my powers of concentration to focus my attention on the first task, i.e., getting the presentation right to the IOC Commission. From mid-February onwards, the Commission were visiting all 5 bidding cities, and it was crucial that we convinced them of the quality of our bid and that we could, indeed, put on the Olympic and Paralympic Games in 2012. Over the three day assessment period, the London Bid Committee would have to show the Commission that we could:

- provide sufficient security;
- raise adequate funding;
- demonstrate a high level of technical ability;
- impress the Commission of our professional competency;
- evidence significant cross party political support.

As the 2012 Olympic and Paralympic Games bidding process was the first summer Games which had to include the staging of the Paralympics as well as the Olympics, we had to get "both" right. It was pointed out to us, that a good Paralympic presentation, would probably not win the Games for London, but a bad one could certainly lose it! So, no pressure there, then?

Some weeks prior to the Commission's scheduled visit, the bid team held a dress rehearsal of the Commission's visit. They arranged for a number of leading experts from all over the world from the Olympic and Paralympic movements to fly to London and be our "mock panel". The bid Team tested out greeting and hosting procedures and facilities, tried the accommodation and conference facility to be used for the Commission's visit, and then presented our bid, and got feedback from the "panel". The team then either changed certain parts of the presentations or strengthened areas thought to be weak or lacking in clarity. We stayed at the Four Seasons Hotel in Canary Wharf and I was greeted on the day of the dummy run by the staff of the hotel, and escorted to my room. I was then, for the first time anywhere in the world, shown what the evacuation procedures were in case of an emergency, and where the fire escape and exits were. The service was immaculate and, when I was asked if they could have done anything more, I commented that an extra touch would have been to have had the information booklet in the bedroom, in an accessible format, i.e. Braille. They listened to what I had said, and the next time I stayed in the hotel, the Braille booklet was in my room!!

On the morning of the first day of the official presentations we were all nervous, as so much depended on the next few hours. The Secretaries of

State for Health and the Home Office attended and gave presentations. Sebastian Coe led the day from the bid team's perspective and, in the afternoon when it was my turn, introduced me to deliver the Paralympic part of the presentation. I had found it, almost impossible in rehearsals to use a script and we planned to use some pictures to emphasise the points I was making. Could I remember the structure and content of the presentation, and could the technical guys get the pictures to match what I was saying? Instead of my usual use of an acronym to keep me on the straight and narrow, I chose to use alliteration as my aid de memoir. I said that the foundation of the Paralympic part of the bid was built on 4 pillars. Each of the pillars began with the letter "p" and then went on to say what each "p" stood for.

The first "p" stood for the Past, i.e. that Britain had a long history, and experience of inclusion and provision of sporting opportunities for people with disabilities. The Stoke Mandeville games which were regarded as the first Paralympics, had started in 1948 and that we had already by 2005 hosted International Games for athletes in wheelchairs, athletes with Cerebral Palsy and for athletes who were blind.

The second "p" stood for People i.e. professionals across the sports who were capable of providing the technical knowhow re the various sports, and the medical expertise re classification.

The third "p" I said stood for the Passion to put on a superb Games. The British loved their sport and would turn out in their thousands to support the athletes. If we were given the responsibility of holding the Games, they would go the extra mile and further to ensure that everything was done to provide not only a wonderful experience for those attending the Paralympics, but for the many thousands of people with disabilities that would be spectators at the Olympics as well.

The fourth "p" was my conviction that the Public would embrace and support the Games like no other host city before. We would have full stadiums, fair and impassioned supporters, and that London with its diversity, would provide a welcome like no other city to the 170 plus countries that would attend.

I finished my presentation, sweating profusely, by saying:

"We have the pedigree, we have the people, we have the passion, and we have the professionalism to stage the best Paralympic Games ever.

Looking back now after the Games in 2012, I feel immensely proud, and a bit relieved, that my claims were proven to be fully justified.

The evening after the presentation Mo joined me in the hotel and brought with her my morning suit to be worn at the Palace the next day.

LOCOG arranged a car for us to travel to the Palace. I was allowed 3 guests at my investiture and had arranged in addition to Mo, for my 85 year old mum and my step dad, to be brought by taxi to the Palace.

On arrival at the Palace, I was introduced to a "Page of the Presence", who then acted as my escort until after I had received my award. He and I chatted for it seemed ages, and then we were briefed as to what to expect during the ceremony.

I would walk up to the Queen, bow, have the medal pinned onto my lapel, chat for the allotted 2 minutes, bow again, and then retreat.

I was trying to think what to say in my 2 minutes when, on being presented, the Queen took the initiative. On seeing my 2012 pin badge, she asked how the bid was going? I said, things were going well and that we were presenting this very week to the Commission, and that I was having dinner with her tomorrow evening at the Palace. My handshake then seemed to be speedier and somewhat firmer than expected, and I was ushered away. The Queen seemed to be laughing as I was ushered off, and I imagined she thought that I was some kind of nutter with delusions of grandeur – having dinner with her indeed!!!

I took my family for dinner in a posh restaurant and I can still hear the words of my mum ringing in my ears, "I'm so proud of you son, and you met the Queen!". I remember having to shush mum when I sat with her in the Palace, whilst others were receiving their gongs. She was getting pretty deaf then, and rather loudly kept saying: "Who are they?" or "What have they done?" I am really pleased that my mum lived long enough to be with me when I got my award, as she died the following year.

The following day I said goodbye to Mo as she set off to work on the tube. I, in the meantime did more presentations, and then travelled by coach to number 10 Downing Street.

On arrival, we were shown into the Cabinet Office, which was a bit cramped as there was about 20 or more of us in there. Tony Blair was hosting, with the leaders of the opposition parties also there to show their support for the bid. We then zoomed back for lunch at the hotel before getting ready for a remarkable evening engagement. Apparently the Queen rarely, if ever, hosts receptions or dinners on a Friday evening, but she agreed to make an exception for the IOC Commission.

I was informed that the Commission group and some of the bid team were to travel to the Palace via river launch and that, if I didn't mind, they thought it might be better if I went by car. I am not sure if they were worried that I would fall in or create a problem, and I remember feeling a bit miffed until they said that Steve Redgrave would be travelling with me in a car. The Olympian with the most Olympic gold medals and me, travelling in a car together, bloody fantastic! When we got to the Palace they had warned them that I was coming but not Steve, and, they honestly didn't know who he was, so I had the incredible experience of introducing him and vouching for him! I remind Steve of this every time I see him.

The dinner at the Palace was fabulous but I was nervous about cutting too hard into the meat, in case I scratched one of the plates. They felt like really expensive porcelain and probably cost £1000 a time! I sat between Ken Livingstone and Prince Phillip's main Aide. I had a conversation with the Prince about his carriage racing and said that I gather that he was still racing. He replied that he was going through his "still" period, i.e. "He was still driving, still drinking, and still alive!"

Prince Phillip's equerry had asked how I was getting back to the hotel after the dinner, and I had replied that as far as I was aware I was going back in the taxi i.e. the same way I came to the Palace. He asked if I would like to have a tactile tour of the dining room and the other areas once the others had gone. I, of course, said yes.

The Queen withdrew and all the other guests filed out to return on the boat they had arrived in. I was then allowed to feel some of the statues and decor in the state dining room and its ante-room. Imagine my shock therefore, when, just as I had my hand up Queen Victoria's nose (the statue that is), Steve Redgrave came rushing up to me and ask what I was doing and that everyone else was waiting for me on the coach. The Queen, Tessa Jowell and Cherie Blair, were standing on the balcony waiting to wave us off! We rushed down and onto the coach and off we went. I think they had completely forgotten that I needed help to get to whatever return transport had been arranged, and had failed to let me know at all what the return arrangements were.

The next day it was such a come down getting on a bus up to the Underground and travelling home on the tube. I had experienced three days like none other in my life. Two trips to the Palace, a visit to No. 10, and presenting to many famous athletes. We had done everything we could do, and the next exciting trip would be to Singapore to do the final presentation and to hear the verdict. I had been told that I was included in the bid team to attend Singapore and I couldn't wait.

Chapter 18

Olympic and Paralympic Success

2005

July 6th 2005 will go down as one of the most memorable and fantastic experiences of my life.

The tension in the room when we gave our bid presentation was almost unbearable, and we felt even greater pressure whilst we sat in the room waiting for the envelope to be opened. Would our lobbying activities be successful, could we have done anything differently or better?

After the presentation to the Commission given in February 2005, we had just seven months to decide what our strategy would be re the composition of our delegation at the IOC meeting, and also what we were going to present. We also had to identify which IOC voting members we knew, and would have contact with in the coming months, and who we might lobby, within the very strict rules we had been briefed on. We decided not to go with the traditional safe approach to the delegation or the presentation. A key feature of our bid dossier was a focus on youth and legacy, and so an inspired decision was made to include 30 young people from a London East End school in the formal delegation, to be sitting in the room in front of the IOC voting Members when we did our stuff.

I had also been included in the 100 strong delegation which each bidding city were allowed, and I was thrilled to be working with so many sporting and business giants. Posh and Becks were there, Daly Thompson, Colin Jackson, Jonathan Edwards, Cathy Freeman, Bobby Charlton, David Hemery, Tanni Grey Thompson, and many more, plus the bid leader Seb Coe. The business delegates included senior representatives from BA, Virgin, EGDF and the banking sector. We, of course, also had politicians represented there – Tessa Jowell, and Ken Livingstone as the Mayor of London. Tony Blair who, despite the fact that he was chairing the G8 summit in the UK the day of the presentations, flew out for 12 hours, and was everywhere, shaking hands and trying to influence people. He was so much in evidence for those few hours that he earned the nickname, "the rash" as he was all over everyone.

I was extremely excited on the day we flew out to Singapore. British Airways, one of the supporters of the bid, had given us an upgrade on our flights and I was to fly Club Class for the first time in my life. I am not sure what was most exciting, the thought of going to Singapore and being part of the presentation, or flying Club for the first time. I think being part of the bid team eventually won, but it was a close thing after experiencing champagne before we had even taken off, and then a bed to relax on during the flight. We stayed in a huge hotel with 73 floors, not that I was impressed by the view! David Beckham hosted the 30 young people for a day, without the press, and this did a great deal to settle them down and get them ready for their part in the final presentation.

The day for the five cities to present soon dawned. The process, it was explained, was that each city went into the chamber with their 100 delegates. They presented their bid and then following questions from the IOC voting members, withdrew. Any IOC voting members from any of the bidding cities did not vote until their city was rejected. The buzz around the conference centre was electric and, whether it was gamesmanship or not, we were constantly being told that the contest was between Paris and Madrid. The questioning by some of the IOC members was however, a bit tactical, and eventually played into London's hands. Prince Albert of Monaco was obviously in favour of the French bid. He asked a question of each of the bidding cities. To the Russians he asked whether Moscow's water transport, which was a key feature of their bid, could cope? Of the Americans, who had problems just before the bid presentation with the availability of their main stadium, he asked whether they anticipated any further issues? He obviously completely discounted London's bid, as when it was our turn he asked whether the weather in London during August would be too wet and would spoil the games? When it came to Madrid, he obviously thought they were the main opposition and asked whether, having had the awful bombings that killed so many people in Spain, could they guarantee that the Madrid Games would be safe?

I am not saying that the disproportionate questioning was the main reason we won, but it certainly helped. Our presentation was stunning, and focussed on the power of sport to change lives. It featured diversity, good gender balance, and the genuine intention to leave a lasting legacy. The French presentation and film came over as a travelogue for Paris as a tourism destination. Moscow was the first city to be voted out, and then New York. It then came down to the nail biting crucial vote to exclude the third city. We watched the voting from a hotel suite and everyone went ballistic when Madrid was voted out.

At this point I had one of the funniest experiences in my life to date. I am not sure if it was a double entendre or a faux pas, but I still burst out laughing when I remember it. Whilst waiting for the final bid we were talking up our chances and saying to each other that now we were in the final 2 we stood a really good chance. The CEO of the BOA and I were talking to Princess Anne, who was urging caution. She said that "one shouldn't count one's chickens before they are hatched" and then went on to say that, as a farmer herself, whose chickens had stopped laying, she knew what she was talking about. The CEO then said, with a straight face, "Ma'am, I think you need a new cock!!!" I spat the glass of wine I was drinking half way across the room and nearly wet myself laughing!

I believe that because of the questioning mentioned above, 2 of the votes previously promised to Paris, were switched to London at the last moment. Of course we did not know this as we filed in to the auditorium with the Paris bid team to hear the final vote. When the IOC platform members arrived on stage, there were about 150 photographers standing opposite the French, and one in front of us. We all thought that the result must have been leaked and began saying things like, well we gave it our best shot, and we couldn't have done any more, etc. etc. I think my heart stopped when Jacques Rogge fumbled the envelope and then eventually said that the 2012 games were to be in, ...

"London".

I don't remember much then other than dancing with Bobby Charlton and Sven Goran Eriksson and being hit on the head by a number of mobile phones that had flown out of people's pockets as they jumped in the air for joy. I then heard my own mobile phone ringing. Would it be the world's press asking me for a quote as a member of the bid team and Chairman of the BPA? No, it was the Romford Recorder (my local paper) asking me if I had heard the news? I gave an incoherent statement and had just started celebrating again when the phone rang once more, perhaps this time the world's press? Again no, it was my cab driver in Northampton who wanted to ensure I had heard the result. I turned my phone off after that.

I then went to the press conference, and the official reception given by the IOC. I must admit I was still really star struck, and couldn't believe I was actually there and had witnessed what I had. I was talking to an IOC member who said that he didn't know what it was like for his country to have won the bid for the games as it was too small, but he had won a few medals in athletics in his time and knew how fantastic it was to win. I had a long chat with him and afterwards said, he was really great, who was he? I didn't wash my hand for a week afterwards when I was told that I had been chatting with, and shaking the hand of, Kip Keino.

We had been briefed about how to act whether we won or lost and were warned not to show any triumphalism regarding the French should we win. One of the party was Daly Thompson, and within minutes of the bid being announced he was wearing a T- shirt which announced to the world that we beat the French at Agincourt in 1185, beat the French at Waterloo in 1815 and now we have beaten the French in 2005 in Singapore!

We then went off to a dinner we had arranged either as a triumphant celebration or a miserable consolation prize. I remember dancing like a maniac, and going from bar to bar as they closed with a gang from the bid team. By four a.m. there were a number of my colleagues who were severely "tired and emotional" and many left to go back to their hotel but not me! I realised at 5 am that I didn't have a clue who the people were that I was still partying with. I think at some stage in the night I had got one of my colleagues to write down my hotel and room number and the final band of good Samaritans eventually took me to my room. If they read this book, firstly many thanks, secondly I hope I didn't say or do anything to embarrass you, and thirdly please get in touch so I can thank you properly! Having arrived back to the room I was not ready to stop drinking and celebrating. I opened my minibar but couldn't work out what bottle was which, so began to take the top off them all and drink them one by one. I had vodka, gin, brandy, orange juice, tonic, beer and much much more. I then decided to phone the world especially those who had doubted the wisdom of the bid and were the most sceptical that we could ever win.

One such call was to my step brother Chris. I apparently harangued him for about 30 minutes but he had the last laugh as the call cost me over £50!

I think I then passed out on the bed happy, drunk and nearly £300 poorer as the result of my numerous phone calls. I am not proud of this example of total excess, but London had won the bid!! I then had a terrible shock, as I lay in bed sweating and hung over, I realised that I had been lying all night on the chocolate that the maid had put on the sheet when they turned the bed down. It had melted and I was petrified that someone might see the dark brown stain on the sheet and think it was something else. I rushed to the bathroom and grabbed my flannel, wet it, and tried to wash the chocolate off the bed sheet, but, it made it worse! One of the greatest moments in my life and I was more worried that someone would think that I had messed the bed.

I eventually rang down to the hotel reception to ask if someone could collect me and take me to lunch and when they arrived, tried to explain what had happened. My embarrassment was soon replaced and reduced to nothing when I heard the news that a number of bombs had gone off in London. We couldn't get much news and virtually all of us assumed that these acts of terrorism were linked to our winning the bid. I later started to realise the enormity of what had happened and also felt sick to my stomach in that all three of the main bombing areas were stations or streets I used almost on a daily basis. BPA's offices were near Russell Square, but I couldn't get through on the phones to see if my staff were safe. Similarly, I had firstly tried to get hold of Mo to see she was safe, but again I couldn't get through.

I remember still that awful feeling of dread and the extremes of emotion, with the elation of the night before of winning the bid, and the feeling of dread and impotence and frustration that I couldn't do anything to help my family or friends, and I was petrified that something had happened to them. I eventually got through and learned that thankfully all were safe. Later that night I left for the airport to fly back. All celebratory receptions had been cancelled for when we arrived and all any of us wanted to do was get home. I got on the plane and accepted my glass of champagne, I could certainly get used to this means of travel. We were then told that there would be a delay and we should await further information. The delay went on and on and when they served us breakfast before we had taken off I thought it must be something fairly serious. With the London bombings on our mind we obviously wondered if that was the cause! It turned out to be a technical fault and at about 5 am, having sat on the plane for 5 hours, we were asked to return to the airport forecourt and return to our hotel. There were five spare seats left on the next flight at 7 am, which went to others in our party including Tessa Jowell , Ken Livingstone and Seb. I ended up sharing a cab with another passenger who eventually helped me to my room, and even did a quick reconnoitre of the facilities with me. Later that morning I then started to phone around to see if any of my other colleagues were still around, as I was alone in a hotel in Singapore and wasn't sure what to do and where to go. I eventually found someone to help and was put on to the same flight the next day and flew back without any further mishaps. I got back home and hugged and kissed Mo with joy and relief. So much had happened in the few days since I had last seen her. My lasting memory of Singapore 2005 is the three "b's":-

The bid

The bombs

The brown stain!

The day after flying back I had to return to earth with a bump as I was having to return to work as Chief Executive of VISION 2020 UK during a crucial time in my tenure.

Chapter 19

VISION 2020 UK: Prevention, Professionalism and Public Awareness

2001-2008

I realised, when first appointed as Development Director to VISION 2020 UK in 2001, that what I needed to do was: to build trust between the various groups; to create a neutral body which would win the confidence of the various bodies in membership; to gain their endorsement of our role and activities; and to ensure that the voice of those at risk of losing their sight, or those living with sight loss, was heard and listened to.

I thought being blind I knew a bit about the sight loss community and service providers but I was wrong. I was both surprised and shocked, at what I found: a lack of trust; real anger from users at the service providers; a sense of arrogance displayed by some of the bigger organisations; a lack of focus on clear campaigning issues; the low profile and awareness of the impact of sight loss on daily living; and a limited sense of how to achieve both political awareness and real change in provision.

Over the first seven years of VISION 2020 UK's existence, I worked hard to build trust between the various bodies and organisations. I was shocked to find when I started that the various professional bodies were just as separate from, and mistrusting of, each other as were the numerous organisations within the voluntary sector.

The early gains I managed to achieve by getting a substantial research grant very early on in VISION 2020 UK's existence, helped immensely to show that there were some real advantages and benefits of working together. I established a number of cross sector forums on specific areas which brought together the different groups to collaborate on a programme with a single joint focus. Such groups looked at research, children's issues, provision of information, technology, learning disability and sight loss, low vision, transport, the provision of emotional support, counselling, and many more.

As the Membership of VISION 2020 UK grew to over 50 organisations, I was able to take on 2 part time staff – one to focus on low vision and the other to help with the growing amount of administration. It became apparent, that, if we wanted to raise the awareness of sight loss prevention issues to the general public, and to obtain political interest and support regarding eye health and vision impairment, we needed to establish a comprehensive UK Vision Strategy that was easily understood and that everyone could sign up to. The RNIB, (the largest organisation in membership of VISION 2020 UK) stepped up to the plate, and offered a significant injection of resources to scope the strategy, consult widely on its content, and to provide the administrative resources needed to create the Strategy.

Over 650 individuals and organisations responded to the consultation and the strategy was launched in 2008. Throughout this period I also developed VISION 2020 UK's website, which provided news of new initiatives, new areas of communication between eye care professionals, those working in social care and the voluntary sector, and most importantly, gave a voice to those people at risk of losing their sight, or were actually living with vision impairment. This collaborative approach was eventually to bear fruit in the establishment in 2012 of an eye health indicator which was the only new indicator as a result of the Health Bill, to be added to the list of health indicators.

Throughout this time, I helped to broker mergers between charities, and enabled or facilitated the combining of parallel or overlapping work programmes under one body. I had been staggered to find on taking up my post that there were over 700 registered charities within the sight loss sector. My work with VISION 2020 UK also brought me into contact with a wide range of vision impaired people and their experiences. I began to realise more fully how lucky I had been in having such a wide range of employment and life opportunities, and just how little sight loss is understood by the general public and by some of the professionals or charity workers supposedly meeting their needs.

A key area, receiving scant, if any attention, was the emotional or counselling needs of the VI. The vast majority of people who lose their sight do so after the age of 50, and the sense of loss on losing your sight is often described as being similar to bereavement. This similarity was brought home to me when I suffered a further loss myself in 2006, when my mum died aged 86. My mum had always been there and had been my rock when I lost my sight. She was always there to fight my battles, or challenge people and explore situations for me. I was so pleased that she had been able to attend the award of my OBE the previous year. My mum had had a tough life growing up in London in the 1930s, and going out to work aged 14. Throughout the war she worked in munitions, and then moved back to London from Northampton, where she had been evacuated. She then worked in the shoe trade in London and rose to the position of manager in a shoe factory in Hackney. It was quite an achievement for a woman to become a manager in the 1950s and she bought our house in the early 1960s which was again quite an achievement. She also had a good sense of humour and sang at the dances or down the pub when she was young. I'd like to think that I inherited much of my mum's determination, humour and possibly even my enjoyment of singing from her.

Chapter 20

A Big Blow to my Confidence and Self-Esteem
2008-09

Someone once said the higher you rise the greater the fall. In my case this occurred in 2008/9.

I, as Chairman of the British Paralympic Association, had worked extensively to build the brand of Paralympics in the UK. We had won the bid and I had to work particularly hard within the LOCOG Board to ensure that Paralympics were included at all stages and not marginalised. We then had our most successful games ever in Beijing, finishing second in the medal table behind China. I had, I thought, worked well with the member organisations within the BPA to gain a view of where we, as an Association, were going in the build-up to the 2012 games and beyond.

The UK Vision Strategy was launched in 2008, and for the first time the sight loss sector had a credible strategy to: eradicate avoidable blindness; ensure that diagnostic and treatment services were both available and improved; and ensure that awareness of sight loss by the public and professionals was enhanced. At the time of launching the Strategy, I was busy helping put the last parts of our preparations for the British team to compete in what was possibly the most difficult competition environment yet, Beijing China.

BPA had established our holding camps in Hong Kong and Macau and competition was scheduled in Hong Kong and Beijing during the games.

As Head of Delegation I was due to support the various individual sports teams at their events and to host Prince Edward, BPA's Patron, as I had done at the previous games in Athens. I would also deal with any major political or disciplinary issues should they arise. In Athens, and again in Beijing I experienced travelling with royalty in the motor cavalcade. When in Athens, Mo acted as my escort, but had to travel in the support car. When we arrived at a venue, Prince Edward got out and, shielded by his escorts, went into the building. Mo had to leg it from the support car, grab me and guide me into the venue and catch up to the Prince. Mo got pretty nippy at leaping out of her car, grabbing me and scuttling off behind HRH. The police guarding him started timing Mo to see how many seconds it took her to get to me and tutted if she slowed down. The Prince could not attend the 2006 Winter Paralympic Games in Torino, but did agree to fly to Hong Kong for the Equestrian events and to Beijing for the other events in 2008.

When we flew out to Beijing, British Airways, which was one of our top sponsors, upgraded Mo and I and others in the party, to Club Class. This was a great start to the trip and we hoped it was a preview of what was to come. The 2008 Games were probably the British Paralympic Team's biggest logistical challenge to date. For the first time our team could take their own horses for the Paralympics, and we had to fly horses, equipment, grooms, vets etc. to Hong Kong, as this was the venue for the Dressage event, whilst all other events were on main land China. This meant we had to split our staffing resources and also arrange additional medical cover should it be necessary. As the sailing team were also based about 250 miles from Beijing it meant we had to split our resources into 3 which was a big challenge. We had also to find the funds needed to take our largest team to date to the Games, fly horses, boats and tons of equipment to China, and still ensure that our athletes got the best support and services ever.

The athletes did us proud, and once again we finished second in the medal table behind China. I managed to attend, and spectate at 14 of the 18 sports we had athletes competing in. The highlight for me, was witnessing our British Paralympic Rowers winning gold and bronze medals in the inaugural Paralympic rowing event.

On our return to Britain we were greeted by Willy Walsh the CEO of BA, and Gordon Brown, the Prime Minister. We had hundreds of supporters clapping the team as they came through, and a full press conference. I was shattered having been away for 3 weeks but so proud of our achievements both sporting and logistical. I was looking forward to having the opportunity to lead the BPA and the team up to and during the 2012 Olympic and Paralympic Games before standing down having completed my 3 terms of Chairmanship.

The elections were to be held in late November 2008, and candidates had a month from our return from China to declare their intentions. I asked one of the other Board Members if he would nominate me and was a bit surprised when he said that he would have to check with the governing body he represented, as there were certain processes to be gone through and, therefore, it might be better if I found someone else to nominate me. I didn't think anything of it and duly found another sport to nominate me. Up until the day nominations closed, I understood I was to be unopposed. I then received a phone call from the Board Member I had originally asked to nominate me who said that he had decided that he would stand against me as Chairman. He had presumably known of his intentions when I contacted him a month earlier, but had been too embarrassed to tell me. There was little time to canvass or undertake electioneering, but I made a point of contacting virtually every sport and voting member to ascertain if there were issues or areas of my Chairmanship that they would like me to explain or change. About half of those I spoke to said they would vote for me and the other half I either had not managed to speak to, or had said they were undecided and would decide on the day.

I then realised that my colleague's decision to stand was not his personal whim but part of an organised movement to deselect me. The day of the AGM and elections arrived. The voting order, looking back, was probably the wrong way round, as the post of Chairman was the first on the ballot paper. As the person Chairing the meeting, the scrutineers brought the results to me, and I could hardly believe my ears. I had lost by 1 vote. Subsequently I realised that 2 of my supporters had not arrived for the meeting and had not arranged for their proxy vote to be cast. I then had to complete the election process and close the meeting. I don't remember much about that final few minutes and felt close to tears at the end when various people came up to me to commiserate.

I had arranged to go to a concert at the Albert Hall with Mo that evening, hopefully to celebrate. I had 2 or 3 hours to kill and on the one hand wanted to be alone and on the other hand, needed to talk to someone to try and make sense of what had happened and why?

In the end I went for a drink with the BPA's Chief Executive, who I think knew more about the move to deselect me than he had let on. I was aware that there was a head of steam building up criticising his performance, and thought I had been the one both tackling the issues and keeping him in check. I was also aware that a fellow Board member had upset a number of the staff and his colleagues, and I had supported him in his decision not to re-stand for the Board. I tried to honestly examine my emotions. I was more hurt I think, that people had not felt able to be honest with me and raise their concerns and issues, and at least give me an opportunity to resolve them. I also felt a bit betrayed that they did not give me an opportunity of going gracefully. I had said that if a credible candidate was proposed I would consider not standing for my final term of office. I am not sure in hindsight that with the lure of the 2012 Games 4 years away, I would have easily stood down, but I might have.

I telephoned Mo to tell her from the bar when my colleague was getting the drinks. I think she was more shocked than I was, if that was possible, and then she was incandescent with anger at my colleagues for their actions. Again, she felt angry, not at the fact that I had not been elected, but the manner in which the de-selection had taken place. I don't recall anything about the concert and remember then trying to rationalise the proceedings of the day by saying things like, "It might be for the best, as at least I would have more time to do other things."

I realised deep down though that I didn't want to do "other things". I had spent 17 years working on establishing BPA as the best national Paralympic body in the world, and creating the Paralympic brand in the UK. Television coverage of the British Team's performances at the various Paralympic Games had massively increased. I had helped to establish the Paralympic World Cup event in Manchester, which was the largest multi-sporting event for athletes with disabilities in the world outside the Paralympics. Despite the significant costs of sending and supporting the largest British team ever at the Paralympics in Beijing, BPA were scheduled to start the financial year post Games, with their highest balance of unrestricted funds.

A week after the election, I attended my last LOCOG Board meeting, as the position on the Board was linked to the chairmanship of BPA. I think my fellow LOCOG Board members were genuinely shocked at my resignation, and said they wanted to retain my knowledge and experience, and would look at whether I could still be involved in some way. I had spent the previous five years as a member of the bid team and then the main LOCOG Board, and suddenly there were some massive gaps in my life.

Christmas, 2008 was not therefore the happiest of occasions. It really started to dawn on me what I had lost and the difference it would make in my life. I had thought of taking early retirement in 2009/10 to be able to devote more time to the London 2012 Games. My Chairmanship of BPA took up virtually all of my spare time and, if I am honest, a bit of my working time too. I didn't have any hobbies, and even my after dinner speaking had been linked to Paralympics GB. What would I do with all this extra time?

Would Mr. Micawber's motto "Something will turn up" once again prove true?

Chapter 21

An Even Bigger Honour

2009

2009 arrived and I celebrated its arrival with mixed emotions. I operate the philosophy in relation to "the New Year" of either celebrating the new one by hoping the coming year would be as good as the previous one, or thanking my lucky stars that the old year had gone and hoping the new one couldn't or wouldn't be as bad.

2008 had seen the successful launch of the UK Vision Strategy, and Britain's most successful Paralympic Games to date, so lots to celebrate. I was no longer Chairman of BPA and no longer a Board Member of LOCOG, so a couple of things to feel hacked off about. It is at these times that well-meaning individuals come out with platitudes such as "well at least you've got your health" They meant well, and what they said may have been true, but I wish they had kept their bloody thoughts to themselves as it didn't help!

I began in 2009 therefore to look around for different things to get involved with, and to increase my involvement in those areas I was already committed to. I had become a Governor of the University of East London in 2006, and as well as being on the main Board, I accepted positions on the Capital Projects Committee, the main Finance and General Purposes

Committee, and the Governance and Search Committee (the latter focussing on recruitment of new Board Members and the overall governance of the university). As someone who has never gone to university I am passionate about ensuring that anyone with the ability should have the opportunity to do so. The University of East London (UEL) is situated in an area with probably the most diverse population in London. The students there come from a very wide range of backgrounds, races and cultures.

I was approached in 2009 to apply for a Board Director's position on the newly formed National Anti-Doping Organisation (NADO). I had been on the advisory body establishing the NADO, and was delighted when my application, following an interview was successful. I was particularly pleased as I felt that I had been appointed for what I could offer in relation to having been an athlete and a sports administrator. It gave me a much needed confidence boost.

About the same time, I was approached by the IT company that I had been working with, to see if I would consider becoming a non-executive Board member of their company. I had been sceptical when people said to me that, as one door closes another opens, but they had been right and 2 unexpected doors had just opened for me.

I suddenly started to get requests for many after dinner speaking engagements, which I had both the time and energy to do.

VISION 2020 UK had expanded to over 54 members, had 17 working groups for me to administer, and I was additionally serving on another 8 committees of other bodies, such as the Royal College of Ophthalmologists. Our annual conference had expanded from a hundred delegates to over 400 and the planning for the next conference began as soon as the previous one had finished.

By May 2009 I was definitely feeling happier, and my self-confidence had been partially restored. I then received a letter from No.10 Downing Street, saying that the Prime Minister, Tony Blair was minded to recommend to the Queen that I receive a CBE for my services to sport. I was shocked, thrilled and a bit surprised at receiving a second honour. When you are passionate about something and then get rewarded for your interest and passion, it seems a bit wrong. At least this time the letter had arrived on my doormat, unlike the previous occasion. When I showed the letter to Mo I did not say anything to her and just handed the letter over. Having read it, the response was not quite what I was expecting. She merely looked up and said:

"What, you?!"

The announcement of the award was made in the Queen's Birthday Honours List in June 2009, which happened to be the day of my Club Metro's National Athletics Championships. I had continued to compete at the games and was entered into the veteran's shot, discus and javelin events. The games had been operating since 1977 and were the only national athletics event for the blind and partially sighted still running on an annual basis. I won one event, came second and third in the other two events. I then rushed off after the event to my niece's silver wedding anniversary celebrations, where they announced my award, which was more than a little embarrassing.

I was invited to collect my CBE in September that year, and set off to the Palace clad in my formal dress suit, but without my top hat. As "top hat" was rhyming slang for someone who looked a bit stupid! I would have had to leave my hat at the door of the Palace anyway, so I decided not to wear one.

When I collected my OBE, I had been separated from Mo on arrival and then introduced to a member of the household, who accompanied me through the ceremony and sat with me in the lounge beforehand. All those to receive MBEs and OBEs were gathered together and as there were about 100 recipients it was quite a festive occasion. When I arrived for the CBE (Commander of the British Empire) it was a different arrangement, with Mo being allowed to remain with me almost up until the ceremony itself. All the CBEs and KBE's (Knight of the British Empire) were gathered together in a small room and there were about 30 of us, with about half a dozen becoming Dames or Sirs. We were then taken through the procedure by a member of the household and were told that Princess Anne was to officiate. I think some of those gathered we're a little disappointed that the Queen was not "doing the Honours", but I was delighted that Princess Anne, my fellow Board Member for over five years, was "doing me".

There had been a bit of a shadow cast on my day however. My brother John and his wife were the other two people in addition to Mo, that were invited to the Palace as my guests. We had arranged to meet up at the Palace, and then I received a phone call whilst I was en route saying that my brother John had collapsed on the train coming to Kings Cross from Cambridge. He was a diabetic so I wondered if it was related to that. June said that the paramedics were with him and that she would ring and leave a message with an update, but that we were to go in and not wait for them. I was worried but there was nothing I could do. I therefore went into the ceremony without knowing what had happened to my brother, which took the edge off things a bit.

When chatting to my escort for the ceremony, he asked whether I would be excited to meet Princess Anne. I said that I was on a committee with her and that I knew her fairly well. I think he thought I was exaggerating or was suffering from delusions of grandeur. When we approached the dais where she was standing, she greeted me by saying:

"Hello Mike, I am so delighted that it is me officiating today".

I replied that I was equally delighted to be receiving the award from her, given our work on the Olympics and Paralympics. We had a couple of minutes of informal chat and then came the handshake and I was off. My escort was impressed that I indeed did know Princess Anne, and remarked that he had never seen that level of informality at the investitures.

We then had the usual round of pictures after the ceremony and met up with family and friends for lunch. My brother had made it to the Palace so everything was wonderful. The medics wanted to take him to hospital and thought his passing out was due to a low pulse plus his diabetes. He made a pretty rapid recovery and insisted that he had to get to the Palace to attend my investiture. I think the ambulance crew were a bit worried about him but he insisted and so, to be on the safe side, they offered to drop him off at the Palace in the ambulance! Talk about upstaging me on my big day – I arrived in a silver Mercedes and he arrives in a bloody ambulance.

After lunch we then went to a bar where I had arranged a champagne reception and about 70 friends and family arrived to celebrate with me.

So as 2009 was drawing to a close, I was certainly in a better mood than at the end of the previous year.

Chapter 22

"Taking stock and yet more challenges"
2009-10

I had planned to retire from work in 2010 when I reached 60, and thus be able to devote even more of my time to supporting Paralympics GB in their approach to the 2012 Games, and of course, working on the Board of 2012 to make the Games the best ever from a disability perspective. Suddenly all of that was gone, and I had begun to develop new interests and commitments.

I still didn't have any real hobbies and was already reading 2 or 3 books a week. I therefore rethought my plans for retirement and decided to put this off for a couple of years and continue to build up a range of activities that I would find challenging and exciting. I was a Governor of the University of East London, and a Board member of the newly formed National Anti-doping Agency (UKAD). I was also finding my non-executive directorship of an IT company, Nemisys, both interesting and challenging, and was enjoying this new experience of working in the private sector.

LOCOG did follow up my departure from the Board by offering me a role as a director of their newly established Diversity Board, which focussed on all of the inclusion issues of both Games from every aspect i.e. employment, contractors, spectator experience, volunteerism, ticketing, information and accessibility - so there was plenty to do. However there was still a big hole in my life, my confidence had been restored to some extent so I decided to apply for a job within LOCOG as the Director of integration. The role involved ensuring that all planning for the Paralympics was integrated into the Olympic planning. The aim was to have the minimum of physical transition of the stadiums from one Games to the other, and that the key staff, such as the venue managers etc., were equally comfortable in Olympic and Paralympic mode. I had been to 12 Paralympic Games – 9 winter and 3 summer – and thought I had the knowledge and skills needed for the post. I felt that this was the door opening that I had been waiting for, and the dream job for me that I would not have been able to apply for if I had still been a director of LOCOG. I went through the preliminary interviews and was shortlisted for the job. It was down to me and another candidate, who was also blind and who had been a multi-medallist at swimming in earlier Games. I won't go into the details of the interview, but basically I came second. I was, of course, disappointed and it felt like yet another rejection from people and organisations that I had worked tirelessly to promote and support. It was in many ways my own fault for putting myself through the hoop once more, and I resolved that I would not put myself through anything like that ever again. I had, reached my sell by date and would content myself with being a spectator at the 2012 Games. Plus I was doing what I could, via the Diversity Board, to ensure that all aspects of inclusion were taken into account. It also stirred up a similar level of resentment in Mo re my experience with BPA. Mo had been a wonderful source of support and encouragement throughout my various sporting ventures, and was upset for me, as she knew how much the London 2012 Games meant to me, and how much I wanted to play an active part in their staging.

I had further causes for regret in early 2010, in that for the first time since the Winter Paralympics started, I would not be attending in any capacity. The 10th Winter Paralympic Games in Vancouver were apparently the best Winter Games ever, with more competitors from more countries than ever before.

I then hit 60 in 2010, and that really focussed my attention on what I wanted to do in the coming months, and especially post the 2012 Games and my eventual retirement from VISION 2020 UK.

In August 2009 I started properly to plan for my retirement. I wanted to be able to do things like walk to the gym or walk through the park to the pub, and realised that this would be difficult just using a white cane. The environment was becoming more and more difficult, with overhanging trees whacking me in the face and covering me in green slime or raindrops. Cars were increasingly using the pavement as their extended parking area, and street furniture was everywhere across the pavements and pedestrian areas. Despite me saying that I would never get a guide dog, I had made enquiries of the Guide Dog Association, been assessed, and in September 2009 went on the waiting list for a dog. They said it could take up to a year to find the right dog, and so it proved.

Chapter 23

Izzy Wizzy Let's Get ..."

2010

Having been involved in combatting prejudice for most of my life, I thought in 2009 it was time that I owned up to my own prejudices. One of which was my prejudice against guide dogs. When I first lost my sight, great emphasis was put on regaining my mobility and becoming a competent white cane user. Such was the mind-set then, that most of us believed that those with good mobility used a cane, and those with crap mobility got a guide dog. Nobody under 18 was eligible to get a guide dog, and therefore I had never met any young or youngish person with a guide dog. This just reinforced my preconception and prejudice that guide dogs were for old, immobile blind people. I loved dogs and had two pet mongrels as a child, and then inherited Mo's mum's dog when she died. Mo had often joked that she knew I didn't have any money when we got married, and only married me to get a guide dog. For over 30 years I had denied her wish, and then in 2009 I seriously began to re-evaluate my mobility options.

I had travelled all over the world using my cane, frequently on my own. I was confident and competent, but increasingly there were encounters with overhanging trees and bushes, collisions with street furniture, and furious encounters with cars parked on the pavement. When travelling on the underground or trains, I had found myself in situations on deserted platforms not knowing where the stairs were or the way out. My journey to the nearest gym, or the only decent pub in the area, was across a park, and the open spaces were difficult to navigate using a cane. I decided that I would inquire re getting a guide dog and hope that my previous attitude or occasional joke wouldn't be held against me. I had said, for example, when speaking at a Guide Dogs for the Blind Association conference, that the sport I most wanted to do was a solo parachute jump. Someone in the audience asked, how I would know when I was going to hit the ground? I, without thinking said, "Well, it's obvious, the guide dog's lead would go slack"! I then dug a further hole for myself when, on hearing the gasps from the audience, I said, "Of course I wouldn't use a new dog"!

The person sent to assess me obviously hadn't been briefed of my misdemeanours and took me on my road test. I had to walk around the area using my stick so they could assess my overall mobility and awareness, plus cane skills. I then had to go on a walk with the assessor acting as the guide dog and with her holding one end of the harness as though it was on the dog, and me holding the other end as though I was being guided by a dog. She was a young attractive trainer, and I considered asking if I could scrap the idea of a dog and just keep the young lady. Mo soon disabused me of this idea and so I was back on the harness, telling the trainer not to sniff and trying to pick up directional changes from her manoeuvring the harness and the lead. I had to get the trainer, metaphorically of course, to sit at kerbs and was just getting worried how the trainer would indicate that she needed a poo or a wee, when we had finished the assessment. I had passed the assessment and was on the list for a guide dog.

The assessment had also included going into extensive details of the work I needed the dog to do. Did I have any preferences re the breed of dog I wanted? Did the dog need good social skills i.e. was I in public situations a lot, and therefore needed a dog that wouldn't be flustered by large crowds or crowded environments? I also tried to convey that I wanted a dog who had a bit of spirit, especially when not on the harness.

I said that I would accept any breed but with the possible exception of a Labradoodle. I had in my mind an image of a Labrador with little pompoms, and although I knew that wasn't what these cross bred dogs looked like, I still couldn't get the image out of my mind.

We went through the training schedule re time off work, and they explained that the likely scenario was that I would go off to a hotel in Essex to train with the dog for up to 3 weeks, and then continue the training back at home. I wasn't too keen on the idea of 3 weeks in a hotel, bored out of my skull, but if that is what it took then so be it.

We eventually agreed that I needed a dog that was:

- fit and liked lots of exercise
- able to behave in public settings like theatres, or when I was doing talks in auditoriums
- not a labradoodle
- had a bit of spirit and was fun
- good with cats
- good with children
- the right size

I was informed a year later that they thought they had the right dog for me, and wanted to know if they could bring her to meet me. I was so excited, it was like going on a first date. Would she like me? Would I like her? Would we have much in common?

The trainer, Krissie, brought her to my home and as soon as she, (the dog that is, not Krissie) came over and sniffed me and then lay near my feet, I knew I had met my second love, after Mo of course. Izzy was a 22 month, old jet black Labrador-Retriever cross. She weighed about 25 kilos so was a bit on the small side, and the trainer was worried in case she was not strong enough for me, and that I couldn't feel her movements through the harness. Otherwise, we seemed to be a perfect match, and they took her off after this initial meeting and said that they would bring her back on 4th September 2010 to settle her in and begin the training. The scheduled hotel training had been cancelled, and I was asked if it was ok for me to be trained individually at home. I couldn't believe my luck, as it meant I could still do my work, around the training, and had the advantage of being at home whilst getting used to the dog on routes and in an area already familiar to me.

At about this time I had been involved in developing a piece of new technology called Ipadio (now called ContactEngine, but more about this later). In essence Ipadio enables anyone, anywhere, by using a mobile phone, to post an audio or video file onto any website. I decided to do a phone blog or phlog about my thinking regarding getting a guide dog, and then my experience of its arrival and the training involved. I called the phlog "One Man and his Dog" and you can still listen to it on www.ipadio.com/phlogs/MikeBrace.

Prior to Izzy arriving, Mo and I went out shopping. I am sure we must have looked like 2 doting grandparents on a spending spree for their first grandchild. We bought beds, (yes plural one for home and one for the caravan), we bought toys (and had great fun choosing between fluffy ducks, elephants, dogs or parrots), we bought bones (for chewing, eating and playing), and spacious baskets (plural again home and caravan), for Izzy to spread out in and survey her domains. I am sure if there had been sets of pink dog booties we would have bought them too! We had also been given a whole range of literature from the Guide Dogs Association. This covered tips re grooming, feeding, things that might be poisonous to the dog, playing with the dog and much more. So it was with a sense of excitement that I awaited the arrival of Izzy on 4th September 2010.

When I opened the door to her and Krissie the trainer, Izzy rushed straight past me and into our lounge. She sniffed around and probably could smell the odour of our two cats that had both died in the preceding 18 months. I was advised to ignore her and just sit down and wait for Izzy to seek me out. This she did within a few minutes and I can't explain the thrill I got when she laid down at my feet. The trainer eventually left after a couple of hours and said she would be back on the Monday to begin our training. Izzy seemed a bit anxious to be left with us but soon settled down.

Mo and I had already had long discussions about house rules and what we would, and would not allow Izzy to do:

We had no children and vowed that we would not allow Izzy to become a child substitute. That intention didn't last long.

We vowed that she was not allowed on the furniture, which we did stick to.

We vowed that we would be strict with her diet and vowed not to feed her scraps, which we have also managed to stick to.

We vowed that we would be in command and dictate what she did, and did not do. That didn't last long either!

We vowed that we would stop her scrounging food and, in particular, picking food up off the streets. Being a Labrador, that proved impossible from the outset!

Someone once said to me that a Labrador lost a bone 3000 years ago and their collective memory has been looking for it ever since. How true!

I won't go into the training in any detail, but I found it both challenging and immensely reassuring. I had been worried that my hard learned mobility skills with my cane would in some way be eroded or reduced, but in fact I found that my orientation skills, directional sense, sound shadow use, and ability to locate objects, were utilised to the full, and if anything enhanced. I went out every day during the training with the trainer and Izzy, and gradually increased the radius of my activities. I started walking with the dog in an area I didn't know and then progressed to routes to the local shops and the tube station. We then went on the underground and trains, and finally buses. I then, at the end of 3 weeks, had to have my driving test, i.e. show that I was in control of the dog and not vice versa. I had Krissie my trainer, and an examiner, follow us on a given route. My test was to walk to the local tube station, get on the District line, change trains to the Hammersmith and City line, exit at Kings Cross, find the exit for the RNIB and end up in its café. Izzy, with a bit of help from me, passed with flying colours. So after 3 weeks we were licensed to go out on our own. The high points in the training were the speed and confidence I could now walk with Izzy, and the low points were learning how to identify when Izzy was weeing or pooing, and if the latter, learning how to put a plastic bag over each hand and then bringing my hands together in a sweeping motion across the ground to where I thought she might have had a dump! I have surprised myself, at how fairly adept at this I have become. I usually allow Mo to do this when we are out, (really good of me I know), just in case I don't notice that I have a hole in the bag, or inadvertently put my hand in the wrong place, and thus find myself, actually, rather than metaphorically, "in the shit".

A couple of times early on I got disorientated and had to seek help in directing Izzy and me back on to the right path. I also had to decide whether the dog was right and I was wrong, or vice versa. A good example of this came some 2 weeks after I qualified with Izzy. One of our regular routes is to the gym which is about 2 miles from home. After walking through the side streets we walk over a railway bridge and then down to the entrance of the park. The park is quite a challenge in that it has lots of open spaces on either side of the footpaths. I went to the gym one evening at about 6.30 and found the path to the gym quite easily and praised Izzy, as it had involved negotiating her way around a gate and finding a footpath diagonally opposite the gate. The office staff in the gym looked after the dog whilst I went off and did my exercise. On the evening in question, I collected the dog at about 8 pm, and set off to do the return journey. We found a gate but I knew it was the wrong one, as Izzy then tried to lead me towards an area with lots of noise and intermittent sounds of applause. I got Izzy to return to the route back to the gym and set off again. I got really annoyed with Izzy when we ended up in the same place and found ourselves walking towards the growing sound of applause. When we did the same thing the third time, I was really frustrated and began to question whether getting a dog was all it was cracked up to be. I heard a passer-by come near me and swallowing my pride, asked them for help. I explained that I was trying to find the path down to the bridge over the stream leading to the main road. The passer-by said that the dog was spot on and that it was straight ahead. I asked therefore what the noise was in front of us i.e. the applause. My mouth must have dropped open with a look of incredulity when the person said: "Oh it's the circus"!

I had not realised that the fields either side of the path were being used for the travelling circus. On the way to the gym the area had been deserted, but by the time I left the gym, the circus was in full flight. I conjured up a mental image of me and Izzy suddenly appearing in the ring, much to everyone's amusement, and Izzy taking off after a horse thinking it was a bloody large dog!

This incident was just one of the topics covered in my Ipadio phlog. I did 30 broadcasts starting with my thoughts before I got Izzy, through describing my elation at getting Izzy and passing my test, and to adjusting to the issues of using a dog independently after qualifying. I had not publicised my phlogs, and mainly did them for my own amusement. Imagine my surprise therefore, at the end of the 30 broadcasts, to find that they had been listened to by 68,000 people in 43 countries! They had, for example, been used in Australia as English as a second language, and I got several emails from would be guide dog owners saying how much they had enjoyed the phlogs and how they had helped to clarify some of the pros and cons of getting a dog.

At the time of writing I have had Izzy six years and they have been full of fun as well as providing me with fantastic freedom of movement. Izzy, I think, is quicker and slicker on my day to day journeys. When tackling new areas, where neither Izzy nor I have been, she is alert, and always seems to enjoy the challenge. It certainly feels much less hazardous and I am completely oblivious of most of the obstacles on the pavements, as Izzy guides me around them with accuracy and ease. In fact I only realised certain things were on the pavement when I decided to use my stick instead of the dog when I decided the dog might be more of a pain rather than a gain.

One problem I had not envisaged was linked to Izzy's name. As part of the training regarding the dog going to the toilet – known in the trade as "spending" – you are told to encourage the dog to spend by telling her to "get busy". I wish I had a fiver for everyone who, when finding out her name then proceeded to say: "oh, Izzy, wizzy let's get ----"

I just manage to stop them saying the last word and avoid the dog crapping on their foot!

She has already provided me with many hilarious moments to add to my after dinner speeches. On one such occasion I was crossing the road near my house and I told Izzy to go right. The command for this is simply "Izzy, right". Imagine my confusion, and then hilarity, when I understood why the woman in front of me said: "How do I tell if he's right, or wrong?" As I tried, and failed, to contain my laughter, I explained to the lady that the dog's name was in fact "Izzy" and I had been asking her to turn right and not asking the woman "Is he right?"!

I can't remember who it was that said when acting, "never perform with children or animals". I was booked to speak at a large conference in Eastbourne, and arrived early to orientate myself on the stage in the theatre where the conference was to be held. I had arranged with Mo, that she would look after Izzy whilst I was on stage, and if necessary, she could take her out of the theatre if she played up. The conference had a second world war theme and the MC was dressed in an A.R.P. warden costume and the lectern was placed in a bunker with sand bags on 3 sides. I felt confident after the run through, that I could enter the stage ok being guided by the MC and walk to the lectern via the open side of the bunker. My hosts then said that they particularly wanted Izzy to accompany me on stage for the photos, and could I therefore bring her on with me? I did have a few qualms about doing this, as on several occasions previously when speaking, Izzy, during my speech, had put both paws on my chest and seemed to plead with me to sit down as she was bored. I had devised a cunning plan whereby when I arrived at a lectern, I would put her lead on the floor and then stand on it to limit her movement. I therefore agreed to their request and duly walked on to the stage with Izzy by my side, found the lectern perfectly, dropped her lead on the floor and put my foot on it. It was a large audience of between 600 and 800 people and I finished my talk feeling that it had been one of my better ones, with the audience laughing loudly in all the right places, and somewhat disconcertingly, sometimes in the wrong ones.

I left the stage to loud applause and re-joined Mo who was crying. I thought wow, I must have been good to move her to that level of emotion, especially when she had heard my talks many times. I then learned, when she could eventually speak, that they were tears of laughter. Apparently, Izzy, once my speech had started had got bored and had stood up. My foot was not on the lead properly and, finding she had a good degree of movement, proceeded to walk over to the sand bags that formed the bunker and lift one off with her teeth and try to undo the laces holding the bag together. Being frustrated with the first bag, she then went over and picked a second one off the pile and set too undoing this one as well. When she decided that she was fed up with that game, she walked around in front of the lectern, and as if noticing the audience for the first time, (Mo swears) Izzy bowed to them!

Izzy, on occasions, lets herself and me down. I was travelling to Cardiff to play cricket in the summer of 2012. The train we were booked on was absolutely heaving and I found out that GB Ladies that day were playing, I think Argentina, in the Olympic women's football tournament, also in Cardiff. A sighted friend and I managed to get the last 2 seats in the carriage and I had told Izzy to lie down under my seat, which she had eventually done. A young child in the seat behind us then proceeded to bawl its head off. I thought to myself, "Just my luck to get a seat in a carriage with a screaming child in it; what a great journey this was going to be". As I chatted to my friend I couldn't help overhearing the mother of the child that was screaming behind me say, "Never mind darling, I'm sure it didn't mean to do it". Alarm bells started to ring with me and I turned and asked, "Has your child's distress got anything to do with my dog?" The mother very politely replied, "Yes I'm afraid so, your dog has crawled under the seat and eaten my son's doughnut!" I reached down to tell Izzy off and she was looking around as if to say "Who me? I don't know anything about it". Unfortunately, the doughnut wrapper was still stuck to her mouth.

I am constantly amazed at people and their attitude towards guide dogs. They seem to think they have super canine powers. For example, I was once asked, "How does the dog know when to cross the road? Can she see the coloured signs on the traffic lights and know when it's safe to go on green?"

I felt like saying, "Don't ask me, ask the dog!"

Chapter 24

Building for Retirement

2010-12

During this period I went part time and got more involved with my voluntary commitments. I took on a few more Committee posts, such as helping to set up a sporting Foundation, and became an advisor establishing sound tennis as part of the LTA's disability tennis programme. I stepped up the after dinner speaking engagements, and set myself a fund-raising target to achieve by the end of 2012. I also embarked on one of my more hair brained schemes, to complete 10 sports in 10 months to raise £10k with 2 other Chief Executives of VI charities, also by the end of 2012! More of that later.

Having set up VISION 2020 UK, I wanted to leave it in the best possible shape for others to carry on the work. I had also decided that I would look at new commitments and be more choosy i.e. do things that I wanted to do and was interested in, rather than something I was familiar with or linked to my being vision impaired.

I then, however made the same mistake for the second time, re not listening to my inner voice re involvement with VI charities!

Having got Izzy in September 2010, I then started to plan in earnest for my retirement. I got agreement from VISION 2020 UK's trustees that I could go part-time from April 2011 and use the savings from my salary to recruit a successor. The work on promoting the UK Vision Strategy was increasingly leading to an integrated approach by the team led by the RNIB and the work VISION 2020 UK were undertaking. The Strategy was owned by, and largely regarded as, VISION 2020 UK's. I therefore tried to establish a co-ordinated leadership of the Strategy, whilst at the same time endeavoured to protect those aspects specific to VISION 2020 UK"s operation.

My directorships of the Nemisys IT company and of UK Anti-Doping (UKAD), were taking up about 3 or 4 days per month of my time, and my Governor role at the University of East London (UEL) a further 3 days per month, so I felt I had more time to devote to some new sporting commitments. I had monthly meetings of the Diversity Board of LOCOG, and all of this fitted in nicely with my going to 3 days a week with VISION 2020 UK. I had it in my mind that I would retire from work completely in the summer of 2012 and would therefore have the first few months of retirement to enjoy the Olympic and Paralympic Games. 2012 would see 2 massively important parts of my life coming together and coming to an end – my working life and completion of my involvement with the Olympics and Paralympics.

I was still worried about whether I would have enough to do once not working so, a bit against my better judgement, did exactly the thing I had vowed not to do, i.e. apply for the chairmanship of a large charity for the vision impaired. I was pleased that I was shortlisted and got to be one of the final 3 interviewed for the role, but I knew when I heard that I hadn't got the job that it was probably too soon for me to have been thinking of aligning myself with another vision impairment charity to fill the gap left by my retirement from VISION 2020 UK. I was certainly disappointed but not devastated, and did not experience the slump in my self confidence that the other non-election or non-appointments had caused.

I still didn't listen to my inner voice however and soon found myself in yet another mess. As a comparatively new guide dog user I had begun to take an interest in issues affecting guide dog owners, especially those affecting travel and equality within the EU. I was asked if I would consider standing as a trustee of the European Guide Dog Federation. I should have trusted my instincts re my earlier decision not to embroil myself in organisations and charities to do with sight loss or vision impairment for at least a year after my retirement from VISION 2020 UK. I attended the AGM of EGDF in Rumania in October 2011 and found myself not only elected onto the Board but nominated as President, and then ended up as Secretary General. The charity was at the end of the first year of administering an EU grant and I spent the first 2 months trying to make sense of the reporting mechanism for the grant, what the details of the programme were and preparing the second year programme to obtain the next year's funding. To say it was in a mess would be an understatement. On the eve of retirement I found myself doing the exact same things as I did when I established VISION 2020 UK. I was doing the finances, writing applications for grants, overseeing the activities we were doing (many of which were in a state of chaos), recruiting and supervising staff etc.

I realised that I had made a mistake by the summer of 2012, and gave notice that I intended to resign at the AGM later that year. I have always relished a challenge and getting EGDF to function more effectively would certainly have been that. Having vowed to myself that I would in future do more of the things I wanted to do, rather than those things I felt compelled to do, I considered that I had let myself down by simply grabbing and responding to the first requests for help I had received. The EGDF commitment felt like I was starting all over again with a full time commitment to a work type activity, and that it was potentially controlling me, instead of vice versa.

Having given myself a good talking to, I started to only consider opportunities or commitments which excited me or I was genuinely interested in. At about the same time as the charity Chairmanship application, I was approached to see if I would help establish a charitable foundation focussed on helping youngsters get started in the sport of judo. The foundation would help fund the cost of judo mats and other equipment throughout the many judo clubs across the UK. I remembered the enjoyment I had got from my judo at the Sobel Centre whilst at North London Polytechnic, and so agreed to become a trustee. Similarly, I was approached by the Lawn Tennis Association's Foundation to sit on an advisory body looking at developing tennis for people with disabilities. My club Metro were pioneering the introduction of sound tennis for the blind, in the UK, and had developed strong links with their counterparts in Japan where the sport had started.

I was still a trustee of the Primary Club and I felt quite a thrill that, as I was coming to the end of my involvement with the Olympics and Paralympics, I was going back to grass roots sport.

I had also increased quite significantly the number of after dinner engagements that I took on. I set myself a target of reaching the milestone of raising half a million pound by the end of 2012 from my speaking engagements. From when I had started, up until early 2012, I had raised over £450k so my target should be within my reach. I was still worried however as to what I would do with myself, post retirement from work and involvement with the Olympics/Paralympics.

I detest gardening, don't collect anything, am not a TV watcher, was already reading 2 books a week. I did want to regain my fitness so planned to go to the gym 3 times a week, and thought that I might try and do some creative writing, hence this second book. Would that be enough though?

Chapter 25

Celebrating a Ruby: no Curry, but our 40th Wedding Anniversary!

2012

Mo and I were married on 1st July 1972 and 2012 saw our 40th anniversary. Having put up with me for 40 years I often thought it is Mo that should be getting the medals and awards not me. She has supported me over the years both during the good times, of which there has been many, and the bad times which, fortunately there have been very few. I still find it amazing that someone has put up with me for 40 years, and I know I owe Mo a very great deal.

I said earlier that much of what I have achieved has been down to hard work on my part, some skill, and a great deal of perseverance, but that a crucial factor has been the support and contributions made by coaches, friends and family. Mo has always been there for me whether it is plodding along on skis, scoring at a cricket match (a sport she dislikes and does not understand), reading my post, correcting my spelling or grammar, or cooking my meals or getting my clothes ready. She has done this whilst doing a job and a wide range of voluntary work. I wouldn't say she never complains, but I do acknowledge she has plenty to complain about!

We normally go on a special holiday to celebrate the bigger anniversaries such as our 25th, 30th etc. but thought that, with the Olympics and Paralympics taking place in July and August 2012, this would be difficult. We decided therefore, to have a big party for family and friends, and then book a cruise for early 2013. We arranged a meal in a local restaurant and invited about 100 people for a sit down meal and then dancing. Much to our surprise, virtually the whole hundred came, and we had a fantastic evening. Four of Mo's five bridesmaids were there, plus my brother who was my best man. School friends going back 50 years came, plus both Mo's and my siblings.

The party occurred a few days before Mo began a six week stint as a Games Maker in the Olympic Village and then a 2 week stint at the Paralympics. So it was with some relief that Mo and I embarked in early January 2013 on a cruise to South America, but I did have to promise Mo, when we were visiting Rio, that I would not be tempted to offer my services for the 2016 Games there. Well I didn't actually promise, I just said I probably wouldn't!

Looking back I have to thank Mo for the 12 years when I was skiing competitively and we didn't have any summer holidays; for the hundreds of hours she has spent holding coats at finishing lines; watching me perform, or listening to my after dinner speeches; for putting up with my obsession with all things technical; for her disturbed nights when I have returned home in the early hours from a speaking engagement; for my insisting on wearing my flares or other inappropriate clothing, despite her protestations; and for keeping her waiting for a guide dog for all that time. I will try and do better over the next 40 years.

CHAPTER 26

Convergence: Celebration: and Challenges

2012

2012 saw very big bits of my life come together. I retired on 28th June, Mo and I celebrated our 40th Wedding anniversary on 1st July. I then attended the Olympics and Paralympics during July, August and September, as a spectator. And I undertook a time consuming sporting challenge i.e. doing ten sports in ten months to raise ten thousand pounds for VISION 2020 UK. I also wanted to reach my fund raising target of half a million pound by December 2012.

By the end of June 2012 I had enjoyed four or five leaving do's. I had set things in motion for the charity to become a charity limited by guarantee, and had arranged for someone to take over my work and move things forward. I was a bit emotional when the speeches highlighted the contribution I had made etc., but felt confident that I had made the right decision to retire, as I wanted to do a number of different things before I was too old. I gave the key note speech at my final VISION 2020 UK annual conference, and even managed to select my own raffle ticket at the reception afterwards. I was just about to put it back when I learned that the prize was a Blackberry with speech, so reconsidered my act of generosity and, accepted the prize!

Thus, free of daily employment for the first time in 44 years, I settled back to enjoy the Olympics and then the Paralympics. I had been involved in firstly bidding for the games, and then preparing for the games over a period of 9 years, and desperately wanted them to be a success. I was invited to test out the facilities of the village prior to its opening, for the athletes, and Izzy and I stayed in one of the accommodation blocks and then ate at the canteen and visited the other facilities onsite. Izzy I think, is the first dog to stay in the village, and she thoroughly enjoyed the distinction with many photos of her inspecting the grass areas and the trees. I then attended the test events in the various stadia and the dummy run of the opening ceremony. I had been chairing a working group advising and lobbying for full inclusion of the needs of blind and partially sighted people, not only as athletes, but as volunteers, spectators and officials. There were problems with accessible ticketing, limited audio description at the Olympic opening and closing ceremonies, poor access to cash withdrawal by the non-provision of accessible ATM's in the Olympic Park, and some problems with obtaining information and programmes in accessible formats, but overwhelmingly, the Games were a massive success from an inclusion and accessibility point of view.

I managed to obtain 2 tickets for the first medal event in the Velodrome and had no problems with accessible seating for my friend, me and my guide dog. One of the most emotional times in my life was standing singing the national anthem waving my 2 four foot union jacks, when Sir Chris Hoy won Britain's first gold medal on the cycle track. Everything that had happened over the previous nine years was put into perspective by that one moment. Despite the knockers, the doubters, the sceptics and the downright miserable, we had delivered the Games, on time, on budget and I think, better than ever before.

Two weeks after the end of the Olympics I attended the opening ceremony of the Paralympic Games. This time there was audio description and, for the first time in attending 13 opening and closing Paralympic Games ceremonies, I had what was happening described to me via an audio link in an earpiece. This service was available to the vision impaired athletes in the stadium, spectators and officials, and was another first for London. I attended 14 events in ten different sports over the 2 weeks and had so many memories to see me through the coming years. I was also asked to present the flowers at a number of medal ceremonies which was a great honour. I felt very emotional when Sir Phillip Craven (the President of the International Paralympic Committee IPC), and I, presented the silver medals and flowers at the wheelchair basketball final in a packed O2 arena.

Even the honour of presenting flowers to medallists was not without its possible amusing and embarrassing moments. One event I was asked to present the flowers for was the archery competition for athletes with amputations. One of the medallists in one of the categories had no arms or legs, and held the bow between the stumps of his legs, and pulled the chord with his teeth! I did have a sweaty moment when trying to work out which category I was presenting to. I eventually asked the medal ceremony organisers whether the 3 Russian athletes I was presenting to actually had arms, and whether I should or should not put my hand out to shake hands, what would I do if there wasn't one there, or theirs came off in mine!

I was so proud at the end that both Games had been the resounding success that they were. Even the weather stayed fine for the Games, and seeing thousands of people with disabilities enjoying the experience of The Olympic Park just as ordinary citizens fully included in a national and international event, was truly a fantastic feeling.

I had been discussing with two Chief Executive colleagues what I/we could do to celebrate my retirement, raise much needed funds for my charity, and in some way, link this all to the staging of the Olympics and

Paralympics. We hit on the bright idea of undertaking ten different sports over a ten month period to raise ten thousand pound each. We called the challenge "The Three Tenners" and offered to sing or not to sing for bonus payments. We would select five team sports and five individual sports from the 30 sports involved in the Olympic and Paralympic programmes. Having given it some thought we selected Boccia, Goal Ball, Cycling (on tandems), sailing and rowing as the team sports. I then chose shooting, track and field, judo and tennis as my individual sports. With all the sporting challenges we laid down some basic criteria i.e. that we would have at least 3 hours basic training in the sport and then a challenge to test our ability or performance. Some of the sports, one or all of us had done before, but many we experienced for the first time.

Boccia and Goal Ball are two team sports from the Paralympics, and we travelled to deepest Essex to undertake our first team sport, Boccia (which is a sport mainly performed by athletes with Cerebral Palsy). The format of the game is similar to boule or pétanque. You have a small ball that acts as the target, and depending on the number playing the game, 2 or more soft sponge balls each, to throw or roll as near to the target ball as possible. We spent several hours practicing and then, took on the reigning Paralympic champions. The maximum that you can win or lose by playing one end in a triples contest is six shots. We lost the first end by six shots but then claimed a minor triumph by only losing the second end by 3 shots.

Goal Ball came next and this time we travelled to a school in Newham which was used by a sports club for young people with disabilities for weekly activities. This sport is played by blind people and involves three players crouching on a court similar to that used in badminton, and then hurling a medicine ball with a bell in it, at the opposing three players. Their job is then to stop the ball by any means possible, and then hurl it back at their opponents. We, (with my 2 colleagues suitably blindfolded) played a number of games and found ourselves competing in the final. We managed to achieve an honourable draw and accepted our medals with pride.

I then undertook my shooting challenge whilst skiing in Norway and managed to win a bronze medal in the biathlon.

In June I undertook the shot, discus and javelin at my club Metro's annual championships.

I then completed a five thousand metre race at the same championships in the windiest conditions I have ever experienced. I know I was tired on the later laps, but at one point as I came around a bend, I swear I was actually held by the wind motionless, and possibly even went backwards!

Five down and five to go. I then started to learn how to play sound tennis which I found really challenging and enjoyable. It is played indoors and the ball is more similar to a softball than a tennis ball. The ball has material that rattles built into it, and the ball is allowed to bounce 3 times each side of the net before you have to play your shot. As the third bounce is really low I am not surprised that the concept of the game started in Japan where many of the blind players are considerably shorter than their British counterparts. Having said that, it is a sport I have really taken to, and plan to continue with into my old age. I can get down to the ball but it is the getting back up that takes longer!

I had done judo when at college, and so completed my individual challenges by attending a local judo club.

The cycling on tandems we did in Surrey and after several hours training our challenge was a circuit of the Olympic cycle course which included a climb of Box Hill. To say we were relieved at the end is an understatement.

The rowing was great fun, as two of us hadn't done this before and trying to get the co-ordination together in the boat was both comic and difficult. We trained in a rowing tank at the rowing centre in the Albert Dock, and then did three timed runs over the 1 kilometre course. I acted as stroke as the others could then see me rowing and try to avoid my oars, or keep in pace with me, whichever was the easier.

The final challenge was sailing and we turned up at a lake in Windsor and were put through our paces in a five man boat on a glorious day in November. We took it in turns steering the boat, crewing it, and I even had the honour of docking it, much to the trepidation of those on the jetty waiting to secure our ropes. We completed the challenge in the time allotted and raised about £7k each for our respective charities i.e. VISION 2020 UK, SeeAbility and the Thomas Pocklington Trust.

We were a bit deflated not to have reached our £10k each target, but highly elated that we had done the ten sports and had a great deal of fun doing them.

With my last talk in 2012, and the fee received for it, I managed to reach my half a million pound fund raising target for my various charities. This gave me an immense sense of achievement and I hope it will not take me as long to raise the next £500,000.

So there I was at the end of 2012, retired after 44 years at work, at the end of my 9 year involvement with the Olympics and 25 year involvement with the Paralympics, having completed my ten sport challenge, celebrated my 40th wedding anniversary, and reached my target of £500k fund raising.

Had my preparation for the next phase of my life been successful, only time will tell?

CHAPTER 27

What Next? Yet More Challenges

2013 and beyond

Looking back over the past 36 years has been very instructive, and perhaps will provide me with good guidelines for what I do in the future. Four years into retirement at the time of writing this book, I think I have almost got the balance right. I still find it difficult not having "things to do" or projects to complete. The pause in activity has, however, enabled me to write this book nearly 36 years after the first book.

One unexpected feeling that has developed and crystallised since retiring is again, that of losing my sense of self or identity. When I had my accident, (as described in my first book "Where There's A Will"), I lost my sense of who I was. One minute I was a healthy 10 year old East End lad playing football with my mates, and the next minute I was "a disabled child". Fifty years later having retired, I have the feeling that I have in some way become diminished especially when meeting people for the first time. When I was working and involved with the Olympics and Paralympics, I felt that I had a job or interests that, when expressed, challenged their perceptions of what people with disability could do. Now, without a job or "role", it feels that I am back to being regarded as a "disabled person"!

I am sure it is similar for anyone retiring. We are so often judged by what we do, and many women experience so many changes in status from being "single", being a "wife" and being a "mum". It does feel however I have, in some way, lost my credentials or additional qualifications for being a person first and disabled second!

What then of my thirst for new challenges, has that been satisfied? No, not a bit.

I have been increasingly involved in the work and running of the University of East London. My time as a Board Member came to an end in July 2015 having completed 9 years as a Governor. I was privileged to be awarded an Honorary Doctorate from UEL in Social Science in November 2015 and I now intend to do all I can to ensure the students have the best opportunities possible to fulfil their dreams and potential.

Similarly, I completed my six years as a Director and Board Member of the UK Anti-Doping agency, UKAD in March 2016. That's eight years with UKAD in total as I had served on the advisory Board which established UKAD from 2008 to 2010. I was particularly excited to be part of this pioneering agency and think it was just coincidence that everything kicked off just as I left! UKAD had just offered to help establish a drug testing programme in Russia and the Sunday Times published an article alleging that UKAD had ignored information about a doctor prescribing drugs to a wide range of athletes! Drug re-testing from Beijing had established a number of positive tests, and results from Sochi are increasingly likely to place the focus back on Russia and their ban at the time of writing from competing in Rio!

The fight against drug cheats will never be over and we may not win, but that is not a reason for not trying.

I have a steady flow of speaking requests and do about 4 a month, and have raised about twenty thousand pounds towards my next half million. I have received 3 honorary degrees which was particularly gratifying given my own lack of formal education. I also received honorary fellowships from the College of Optometrists and from the Royal College of Ophthalmologists, so I suppose I can diagnose a problem by giving someone a sight test and then operate on them as an Ophthalmologist – only kidding!

I am now non-executive Chairman of Nemisys, a web design company, and an investor in Ipadio (now Contact Engine) and promote it whenever I can. I am really enjoying being a trustee of the Primary Club, the British Judo Council Foundation, and have enjoyed being a mentor for another person with vision impairment who is seeking to develop his career and leadership capabilities.

My club Metro are celebrating their 40th anniversary athletics meeting at the original stadium in Mile End and Izzy and I are travelling for the first time abroad to Norway so look out for more incidents and phlogs on our return. I am Chairing my local Authority's Vision Strategy Group, and through this involvement have become a Director of East London Vision. This is an umbrella group covering the 7 East London Boroughs, and much like my work with VISION 2020 UK, I am endeavouring to get all of the various health, social care and voluntary sector bodies within East London to work more closely together. Again, through this latter involvement, I have become a member of the London Eye Health Network Steering Group and am a lay assessor for the National Institute of Health Research.

Writing this book has given me a taste for trying to do some creative writing, perhaps some thirty minute theatre scripts, or a novel, who knows?

I am sure I will become a very reluctant gardener if Mo has anything to do with it! 5 years ago we bought a large new static caravan in Northamptonshire, which also has a large garden, so I think I might be doubly busy digging, hoeing or whatever gardeners do. My main complaint is that I can't see what is growing and get no benefit from the beauty or colour, and just get the aching back, sweaty body and callused hands!

I am enjoying keeping fit at the gym and having long walks with Izzy, and championing my various charities. I am thinking of doing the "end to end" cycle ride on a tandem for my 70th birthday in 2020. I haven't told Mo yet so I would be obliged if you didn't say anything to her. I have taken up sound tennis and hope to get good enough to compete at it in the near future. I suspect this will depend as much on whether my knees hold out and I can still move around, as to whether I manage to acquire the necessary skills. I plan to take up golf and have acquired a set of left-handed golf clubs.

My speaking engagements are giving me the opportunity to travel a bit, and most importantly, reach new audiences and hopefully to influence their view of disability.

When I look back to the experience of being featured on "This is Your Life" 34 years ago, I thank God that my fears then, as to whether my life was complete and I had experienced everything that I was going to, were completely unfounded.

Eddie Edwards's recent biopic made me reflect on how we were regarded when we first started our fundraising efforts for the Paralympic ski team. Initially our efforts to gain publicity and funding received similar responses to Eddie the Eagle, with many people saying that Brits shouldn't be cross country skiing at all, let alone that we were also blind ...!

But as it turned out, I have been so lucky to have the family and friends that I have, to have had so many opportunities at work and play and to have met so many fantastic enablers that have given me so much fun, and the opportunities to extend my abilities and understand my disability.

Who knows what's around the corner, and what the next 30 plus years have in store for me? As long as it is challenging and interesting, and hopefully I get a chance to touch people's lives and change their perceptions, then I am ready and excited to "M-brace the future" (no pun intended).

As I always say at the end of my talks:

"Disability is a state of mind, my state, and your minds! You can't change my state, but hopefully, I've said something that has changed your mind?"

APPENDIX

Can you help Mike with his fundraising?

Want to help Mike raise his next half million pounds for charity? Why not book him to talk at your society or dinner?

Read more about Mike at www.mikebrace.co.uk

Mike can be contacted on mike@mikebrace.co.uk

46959696R00078

Printed in Poland
by Amazon Fulfillment
Poland Sp. z o.o., Wrocław